D0343181

TOM PETERS
ESSENTIALS
DESIGN

THE ESSENTIALS SERIES IS ADAPTED FROM *RE-IMAGINE!*

LONDON, NEW YORK, MUNICH,
MELBOURNE, AND DELHI

Editor **Michael Slind**
Project Art Editor **Jason Godfrey at Godfrey Design**
Senior Editor **Dawn Henderson**
DTP Design and Reproduction **Adam Walker**
Production Controller **Luca Frassinetti**
Managing Editor **Julie Oughton**
Managing Art Editor **Heather McCarry**
Publishing Manager **Adèle Hayward**
Category Publisher **Stephanie Jackson**
Art Director **Peter Luff**

First published in the USA in 2005 by
DK Publishing, Inc.
375 Hudson Street, New York, NY 10014

First published in Great Britain in 2005 by
Dorling Kindersley Limited,
80 Strand, London WC2R 0RL
A Penguin Company

2 4 6 8 10 9 7 5 3 1

DK books are available at special discounts for bulk purchases for sales promotions,
premiums, fund-raising, or educational use. For details contact: SpecialSales@dk.com

A Cataloging-in-Publication record for this book
is available from the Library of Congress.
(US) ISBN 0-7566-1054-0

A CIP catalog record for this book
is available from the British Library.
(UK) ISBN 1 4053 0258 5

Reproduced by Colourscan, Singapore
Printed and bound in Italy by Graphicom

Discover more at
www.dk.com

CONTENTS

INTRODUCTION

Re-imagining ... What's Essential

Fall 2003. I publish my Big Book ... *Business Excellence in a Disruptive Age*. It is, since the publication of *In Search of Excellen*ce in 1982, my most ambitious attempt to state comprehensively ... What Business Is. (Or Could Be.) (Or *Must* Be.)

The year following, 2004. While traveling to promote the book ... and while keeping up with my usual speaking and consulting schedule... I note a steadily increasing drumbeat. A drumbeat of consternation around the issue of "outsourcing." (Or "off-shoring.") Jobs going to India. Or China. Or just ... Somewhere Else.

What is to be done? How can people cope ... with the specter of ... massive job shrinkage? My (nutshell) answer: Job shrinkage is inevitable. Whether because of outsourcing or automation (which, long-term, may be a bigger deal than outsourcing), you can't count on any job being "there for you." What you can do is find ways to move yourself and your company Up the Value Chain ... and into the heart and soul of the New Economy.

Summer 2005. I publish a series of four quick and to-the-point books, one of which you now hold in your hand. The "Essentials" is what the series is called. As in: Here are the essential things you *must* know ... as you strive to *act* ... in this unstable, up-tempo, outsourcing-addled, out-of-this-world age.

New Economy, New Mandate, New Story

A lot of yogurt has hit the fan. In the near term, globalization continues to be a mixed blessing—a worthy end point, but messy and uneven to the extreme in its immediate impact. Waves of technological change engulf us—and confuse us. Corporate scandals erupt. Once-mighty titans (namely: big companies and the CEOs who lead them) fall from their lofty perches

And yet ... there *is* a New Economy.

Would you change places with your grandfather? Would you want to work 11 brutal hours a day ... in yesterday's Bethlehem Steel mill, or a Ford Motor Company factory circa 1935? Not me. Nor would I change places with my father ... who labored in a white-collar sweatshop, at the same company, in the same building, for 41 l-o-n-g years.

A workplace revolution is under way. No sensible person expects to spend a lifetime in a single corporation anymore. Some call this shift the "end of corporate responsibility." I call it ... the Beginning of Renewed Individual Responsibility. An extraordinary opportunity to take charge of our own lives.

Put me in charge! Make me Chairman and CEO and President and COO of Tom Inc.

That's what I ask! (Beg, in fact.)

I *love* business at its best. When it aims to foster growth and deliver exciting services to its clients and exciting opportunities to its employees. I especially *love* business at this moment of flux. This truly magical, albeit in many ways terrifying, moment.

I'm no Pollyanna. I've been around. (And then around.) My rose-colored glasses were long ago ground to powder by brutal reality.

Yet I am hopeful. Not hopeful that human beings will become more benign ... or that evil will evaporate ... or that greed will be regulated out of existence. But I am hopeful that in the New Economy people will see the power that comes from taking responsibility for their professional lives. And I am hopeful that they also will find pleasure in unleashing their instinctive curiosity and creativity.

The harsh news: This is Not Optional. The microchip will colonize all rote activities. And we will have to scramble to reinvent ourselves—as we did when we came off the farm and went into the factory, and then as we were ejected from the factory and delivered to the white-collar towers.

The exciting news (as I see it, anyway): This is Not Optional. The reinvented *you* and the reinvented *me* will have no choice but to scramble and add value in some meaningful way.

The Back-Story: A Tale/Trail of Disruption

Each book in the series builds on a central premise—the same premise that I propounded in the early chapters of *Re-imagine*! Herewith, an Executive Summary of that Progression of Ideas.

1. All bets are off. It is the foremost task—and responsibility—of our generation to re-imagine our enterprises and institutions, public and private. Rather strong rhetoric. But I believe it. The fundamental nature of the change now in progress has caught us off-stride and on our heels. No aspect of the way our institutions operate can be allowed to go unexamined. Or unchanged.

2. We are in a ... Brawl with No Rules. Business, politics, and, indeed, the essential nature of human interchange have come unglued. We have to make things up as we go along. (Success = SAV = "Screw Around Vigorously.") ("Fail. Forward. Fast.") Yesterday's strictures and structures leave us laughably—and tragically—unprepared for this Brawl with No Rules. From al Qaeda to Wal*Mart, new entrants on the world stage have flummoxed regnant institutions and their leaders.

3. Incrementalism is *Out*. Destruction is *In*. "Continuous improvement," the lead mantra of 1980s management, is now downright dangerous. All or nothing. ("Control. Alt. Delete.") We must gut the innards of our enterprises before new competitors do it for us—and to us.

4. InfoTech changes everything. There is no higher priority than the Total Transformation of all business practice to e-business practice. The new technologies are ... The Real Thing. The IT Revolution is in its infancy. And yet it has already changed the rules—changed them so fundamentally that years and years will pass before we can begin talking about constructing a new rule book.

5. Ninety percent of white-collar jobs as we know them (and, ultimately, 90 percent of all jobs as we know them) will be disemboweled in the next 15 years. Done. Gone. Kaput. Between the microprocessor, 60/60/24/7 connectivity, and outsourcing to developing countries, the developed nations' white-collar jobs are ... doomed. Time frame? Zero to 15 or 20 years. How confident am I on this point? Totally.

6. "Winners" (survivors!) will become *de facto* bosses of Me Inc. Self-reliance will, of necessity, replace corporate cosseting. Old-style corporate security is evaporating. Upshot: Free the cubicle slaves! The only defense is a good offense! Hackneyed? Sure. But no less true for being so. A scary ... but also immensely exciting ... New Age of Self-Reliance is being birthed before our eyes. Hurray!

Story Time—for a Storied Time

Building on that premise, each book in this series tells a story—a saga of how we will survive (and, perhaps, go beyond survival) in this Dizzy, Disruptive Age.

A Story about *Leadership*. Command-and-control management ... "leadership" from on high ... is obsolete. New Leadership draws on a new skill set—the hallmarks of which are improvisation and inspiration. It taps into the unique leadership attributes of women. It cultivates Great Talent by creating a Great Place to Work.

A Story about *Design*. New Value-Added derives less and less from "product" or "service" quality, and more and more from ... Something More. Something called "Experiences." Something called "Branding." Something called "Design."

A Story about *Talent*. It's a Brand You World. "Lifetime employment" at a corporation (aka "cubicle slavery") is out. Lifetime self-reinvention is in. The only fool-proof source of job security is … your talent. And your talent will express itself by building a scintillating portfolio of WOW Projects and by Thinking Weird (as these weird, wild times demand).

A Story about *Trends*. Where, amid so much flux and discontinuity, are the Big Market Opportunities? They are hiding in plain sight. Go where they buyers are and where the money is—among women and among aging boomers.

The Story Re-imagined: What's New

To tell these stories, I have adapted selected chapters from *Re-imagine!* As necessary or as I've seen fit, I have nipped and tucked and otherwise revised each chapter throughout. Plus, I have salted the tale here and there with new supporting material.

In addition, I—along with the folks at my publisher, Dorling Kindersley—have re-imagined the the look-and-feel of each book from the inside-out. With *Re-imagine!*, we set out to re-invent the business book. We wanted to tell the story of a world of enterprise that is bursting at the seams with revolutionary possibility, and so we created a book that bursts forth with Passion and Energy and Color. For the Essentials series, we have retained those qualities, but we have also stripped the design of these books down to its … essentials. Same Passion. Same Energy. Same Color. All in a format that fits in your hand … and meets (we believe) your essential needs.

Two new features punctuate and amplify the Story Being Told.

First, capping each chapter is a list of "Top 10 To-Dos"—a one-page digest of the chapter in the form of action items that will inspire you to Do Something … right away. Here again, the emphasis is on drilling down to … what's essential.

Second, between certain chapters we include highlights from interviews with "Cool Friends"—smart people whose work has helped make me smarter. Their voices add insights that give texture to the story. Full-text versions of these and other interviews appear on my Web site (www.tompeters.com).

Last Words ...

I don't expect you'll agree with everything that I say in this book. But I hope that when you disagree ... you will disagree *angrily*. That you will be so pissed off that you'll ... Do Something.

DOING SOMETHING. That's the essential idea, isn't it? The moral of my story—the story of What's Essential about the present moment in business—comes in the form of a tombstone. It's a tombstone that bears the epitaph that I most hope to avoid. To wit:

𝔗𝔥𝔬𝔪𝔞𝔰 𝔍. 𝔓𝔢𝔱𝔢𝔯𝔰
1942–𝔚𝔥𝔢𝔫𝔢𝔟𝔢𝔯
𝔥𝔢 𝔴𝔬𝔲𝔩𝔡 𝔥𝔞𝔟𝔢 𝔡𝔬𝔫𝔢 𝔰𝔬𝔪𝔢 𝔯𝔢𝔞𝔩𝔩𝔶 𝔠𝔬𝔬𝔩 𝔰𝔱𝔲𝔣𝔣 ...
𝔟𝔲𝔱 𝔥𝔦𝔰 𝔟𝔬𝔰𝔰 𝔴𝔬𝔲𝔩𝔡𝔫'𝔱 𝔩𝔢𝔱 𝔥𝔦𝔪

Meanwhile, I know exactly how I *do* want my tombstone to read:

𝔗𝔥𝔬𝔪𝔞𝔰 𝔍. 𝔓𝔢𝔱𝔢𝔯𝔰
1942–𝔚𝔥𝔢𝔫𝔢𝔟𝔢𝔯
𝔥𝔢 𝔴𝔞𝔰 𝔞 𝔭𝔩𝔞𝔶𝔢𝔯!

Not "He got rich." Not "He became famous." Not even "He got things right." Rather: "He was a player." In other words: He did *not* sit on the sidelines ... and watch the world go by ... as it was undergoing the most profound shift of basic premises in the last several hundred years (if not the last thousand years).

Agree or disagree with me on anything else, but if you have a grain of integrity or spirit or spunk or verve or nerve, you must agree with me on this: Getting off the sidelines—Being a Player—is Not Optional.

No. In fact, Being a Player is ... *Essential!*

1

DESIGN: THE "SOUL" OF NEW ENTERPRISE

Contrasts

Was	Is
Design-challenged company	Design-driven company
Design as cost center	Design as value generator
Design is an after-the-fact "prettifying" element	Design is the heart and soul of an enterprise
Designers labor away in a peripheral department	Designers have a seat at the Head Table (Board of Directors)
Design is outsourced to this or that vendor	Design is integral to the entire organization
Drab HQ (Just a place to work: You punch out ASAP)	Cool HQ (A place to create: You come early and stay late)
Boring, "businesslike"	Exciting, "WOW-like"
Brooks Brothers	Armani
Frowns	Smiles

!Rant

We are not prepared ...

We consider "design" ... when we consider it at all ... to be about "patina" ... "a little something on top." • But we must appreciate that **design is the** ... **SEAT OF THE SOUL**.

We view design as a "finishing-off process." • But **WE MUST UNDERSTAND THAT A THOROUGHGOING "DESIGN SENSIBILITY" CAN EFFECTIVELY DRIVE ENTERPRISE STRATEGY**—and cease to be a neglected second cousin.

We think of designers ... when we think of them at all ... as odd ducks who should be confined to their cubicles, far away from the strategy "war room." • Instead, we must **INVITE DESIGNERS** to sit next to the CEO **AT THE BOARDROOM TABLE**.

!Vision

I imagine ...

A Finance "Department" ... **with a Musician ... a Poet ... an Artist ... an Actress ... and an Anthropologist.** (As well as some Numbers Dudes.) • This "Department" stands for **ACCURACY AND INTEGRITY.** But it is also a ... Scintillating Business Partner. **Its members are not drones.** • They do not hide behind dense, obscure Excel spreadsheets filled with arcane figures. • **THEY ARE EXCITING. THEIR IDEAS ARE EXCITING.** • Their presentations are exciting. And Clear. And Beautiful. • **BECAUSE THESE NEW-BREED "FINANCE PEOPLE" ARE ... DESIGN DRIVEN.**

Design is about "soul"

It's Got Soul

I, not the Greek philosophers, have discovered the "Seat of the Soul."

At least in enterprise.

And it is ... Great Design.

Does saying that make me arrogant?

Yes.

So what?

Hey, I've got Steve Jobs on my side. "In most people's vocabularies, design means veneer," says the genius behind Apple, Next, Pixar ... and Apple again. "Nothing could be further from the meaning of design. Design is the fundamental soul of a man-made creation."

Damn few "get it." Most people consider design a surface thing, a "prettifying" thing, an after-the-fact cosmetic-makeover thing. But in Apple-land ... and Sony-land and Nokia-land ... it is the antithesis of all that.

Design is about "soul."

Design comes first.

Design drives and defines the enterprise and its fundamental value proposition.

I, alone among the "management gurus," write extensively about design.

Why?

IT TURNS ME ON.

Design Turn-On: Smooth Sailing

I grew up on the water. Sullivan's Cove, on the Severn River, near Annapolis, Maryland.

Rivers are in my blood. (And in my soul.)

So I return from a trip to my old stomping ground ... and my back aches. (It always does.) Yet my suitcase is three pounds heavier than it needs to be.

Why?

design

!

the "soul" of new enterprise

PASSION POINT
Design—along with Design Mindfulness—is the Mount Everest of "intellectual capital."

It is—like Music, like Art—the pinnacle of Human Accomplishment. It involves nothing less than bringing to bear on the

task at hand ... what it means to be fully engaged and fully human.

The turnbuckle
I carry with me. I got
it at Fawcett's, Annapolis's
premier yacht supply store. (When I
was a kid. And still today, when I'm not.)

A turnbuckle tightens rigging. It's an
8-inch-long, $60 piece of chrome sailboat
hardware. It's also ... beautiful. (Just look at the
photo above.)

Confession time: *I fondle it as I write.*

Design Turn-Off: Hotel Hell

I'm on the road about 200 nights a year. That's extreme.
But a lot of us surely score 100 "nights away" per year.

Most of us—I suspect—hit the hotel room, sigh twice,
plug in, and get to work on our "second day of work."

Fact is, I arrive in the room ... unzip my bag ... get
out my balls of tangled wires ... crawl around on the floor
... plug in ... and ... SPEND FOUR TO SIX HOURS OF
THE NEXT TWELVE ... ONLINE OR SCREWING AROUND
WITH TOMORROW'S POWERPOINT PRESENTATION.

Problem: *Only 1 hotel in 10 or 15 "gets it."*

I'm *not* talking DSL.
I'm talking MAB:
My Aching Back.

I am PISSED OFF at hotels that provide great
couches and armoires ... which I *never* use ... but offer ...
CRAPPY DESKS ... WITH UNBELIEVABLY CRAPPY DESK
CHAIRS ... CHAIRS THAT RUIN MY BODY.

Message to hotel "stylists": YOUR HOTEL ROOM IS
MY "OFFICE." (More than my "Official Office.") PLEASE

... RESPECT THAT FACT! PLEASE ... RESPECT MY ACHING BODY! (Do so, and you'll earn my custom. And my undying affection.)

DESIGN FOR WINNING

Hotels are a bell-wether, design-wise. And some are starting to "get it." Virginia Postrel, writing in her 2003 book, The Substance of Style. How the Rise of Aesthetic Value Is Remaking Commerce, Culture, and Consciousness: *"Elaborating on the techniques of one-of-a-kind boutique hotels, Starwood Hotels & Resorts [W, Sheraton, Westin] has adopted a strategy of 'Winning by design.' "*

"Design" Defined: A PowerPoint Epiphany

Defining "design": It ain't easy. It *is* important.

In late 2000 I was charged with keynoting a major design conference. I spent an eternity on my presentation. But as the moment of truth approached, I still was unhappy. Extremely unhappy. I'd been working at this "damn design thing" for years. And I still hadn't figured out why it had gotten so, so far under my skin.

Finally, at about 5 a.m. on the day the conference opened, I got up and tapped out some text for a few PowerPoint slides.

Here's what erupted onto the slides:

1. *Design "is"* ... *WHAT AND WHY I LOVE. L-O-V-E.*

Design is not about "like." It's not about "dislike." It's about real passion ... strong emotion ... deep attachment.

At design conferences, I discovered, designers invariably bring along their favorite toys. It took forever for me to figure out what to bring. In the end, all I had to do was

look in my suitcase. And there they were—a couple of boxes of them. Ziplocs!

Ziplocs: Couldn't live without them. If "they" quit making them, I would probably pull the last one over my head—and sign off. It's "just a plastic bag," you say? But not so! It has a million uses. It has spectacular design.

Brilliant!

design

2. *Design is … WHY I GET MAD. M-A-D.*
Design is about stuff that makes me chortle. And it's about stuff that makes me … *scream.*

As I said, I spend probably 200 nights a year in hotels. And I'm not as young as I used to be. I've worn glasses for about 20 years. (*Tri*focals, these days.) But I don't wear glasses when I'm in the … bathroom. (Who does?) Hence nothing on earth pisses me off more than … shampoo bottles on which the word "shampoo" is in such fine print that you can't read it.

I don't merely find this experience "unpleasant." It flat-out … *pisses me off.*

3. *Hypothesis: DESIGN IS THE PRINCIPAL DIFFERENCE BETWEEN … LOVE AND HATE!*
It took me a dozen years to arrive at that insight. It's pretty blunt. But I think it was worth the dozen-year wait—because that is precisely what I believe.

Corollary hypothesis:

It's not about "sorta."

the "soul" of new enterprise

FEELING—GROOVY!
According to a study published in the *Journal of Advertising Research*, emotions are twice as important as "facts" in the process by which people make buying decisions. The study involved more than 23,000 U.S. consumers, exposed these subjects to 240 advertising messages, and covered 13 categories of goods (with emotion trumping "fact" in *all* 13 categories).

Design IS WHAT and why I

Hence I began my presentation to that Design Conference in 2000 as follows:

"I am a design fanatic. Though not 'artistic,' I love 'cool stuff.' But it goes much, much further ... far beyond the personal. 'Design' has become a ... PROFESSIONAL OBSESSION. I SIMPLY BELIEVE THAT DESIGN— per se—IS THE PRINCIPAL REASON FOR EMOTIONAL ATTACHMENT (or detachment) RELATIVE TO A PRODUCT OR SERVICE OR EXPERIENCE. Design, as I see it, is arguably the NO.1 DETERMINANT of whether a product-service-experience stands out—or does not. Furthermore, it's 'one of those things' that damn few enterprises put—consistently—on the Front Burner."

> **PREVIEW OF COMING "EXPERIENCE"**
> *A word about that word:* experience. *For me, as I explain below, "design" encompasses not just manufactured goods ... but a company's entire Value Proposition. In other words: every aspect, tangible and otherwise, of the* experience *on offer by the company.*
>
> *I elaborate on this idea at great length in Chapter 3: "Design in Action: Providing Memorable Experiences."*

I wish, somehow, I could magically take you on my adventure. My adventure of "Love" and "Hate" and "Never Neutral." My conclusion that design is right at the Heart (and SOUL) of business.

Design Myths I: What FedEx Knows That You Maybe Don't

Think about design, and you probably think about ... a Ferrari. A Rolex. Perhaps an iMAC. That is: lumps of stuff, not (mere?) services.

Baloney.

BEST BED

I'm hooked ... on the Westin Heavenly Bed.

What do you do in a hotel room? You've marched through a full day of meetings. You're zonked. You get to the room. You check your email and work on your next presentation. You go to sleep. You get up. You go to some more meetings. Thus, the "sleeping part" is right at the center of it. And I, for one, don't believe that man or woman was meant to sleep under polyester.

Those Westin beds? Fabulous! Westin knows it! And exploits it! Great beds! Great duvets! Great marketing ploy!

DESIGN is about

SERVICES

as much as it is about

lumps

!

We are (A-L-L) designers

I.D. [International Design] magazine published in 1999 its first, and so far only, list of the 40 "most design-driven companies in America." To be sure, Apple Computer was on the list. As was Caterpillar. Gillette. IBM. New Balance. Patagonia. 3M.

More interesting to me, fully half the companies were ... service companies. Amazon.com made the list. So did Bloomberg. Also: Federal Express. CNN. Disney. Martha Stewart. Nickelodeon. The New York Yankees. Even ... The Church of Jesus Christ of Latter-day Saints.

Message: *Design is about services as much as it is about lumps.*

And that goes for internal services as well as external services. Design is about ... the Purchasing Department. The Training Department. The Finance Department.

Presentation of a financial report is as much a "design thing" as is the creation of a sexy-looking product at John Deere. (Yup, Deere long ago made "cool" and "farm implement" synonymous. And shareholders clip fat coupons as a result.)

Big Message: *We are all (A-L-L) designers.* Each and every one of us gives off dozens—probably hundreds, perhaps more—of "design cues" every day. In the way we present ourselves. In our project "output." And so on.

Thus: Design is *not* about lumpy objects. Design is not the provenance of the New Product Development Department ... or the Marketing Department ... alone.

Design Myths II: What Tar-zhay Knows That You Maybe Don't

Think again about that Ferrari. That Rolex. Even that iMac. These are iconic triumphs of design, right? And they're not only lumps—they're expensive lumps. But design is not restricted to $79,000 sports cars. Or even to funky $1,000 computers. If ever we needed evidence of that point, then the startling rise—in the face of Wal*Mart's awesome prowess—of Target (aka Tar-zhay) is proof positive of design's potentially Transforming Role. *Time* magazine called Target "the champion of America's new design democracy." *Advertising Age* awarded Target its coveted Marketer of the Year award in 2000.

Target *was* a discounter. Target *is* a discounter. Target plans to be a discounter from now until hell freezes over. Nonetheless, Target has gone, hammer and tong, after design-as-exceptional-differentiator—and in doing so, has proven once and for all (I hope) that "discounter" and "cheap crap" do not have to be synonymous.

TARGET OF OPPORTUNITY

I just couldn't help myself. In a meeting with the senior merchandising staff of a huge discount retailer, I let loose my wrath: "Target has done it. So what's holding you back? You have incredible purchasing might. Flatly demand of your vendors that each and every product that you put on your shelf, mundane or grand, be a Pure Aesthetic Joy. Why not be as tough on your vendors about design as you are about price?"

Yes, why not? (Damn it.)

Gillette is another leader in demonstrating that Awesome Design can be applied to relatively inexpensive items. Consider the Sensor. It redefined women's shaving. And when we thought we'd seen the last word on men's

design ! the "soul" of new enterprise

BRUSHING UP!

Virginia Postrel, writing in *The Substance of Style:* "The lowliest household tool has become an object of color, texture, personality, whimsy, even elegance. Dozens, probably hundreds, of distinctively designed toilet-brush sets are available—functional, flamboyant, modern, mahogany. For about five bucks, you can buy Rubbermaid's basic plastic bowl brush with caddy, which comes in seven different colors, to hide the bristles and keep the drips off the floor. For $8 you can take home a Michael Graves brush from Target, with a rounded blue handle and translucent white container. At $14, you can have an OXO brush, sleek and modern in a hard, shiny white plastic holder that opens as smoothly as the bay door on a science-fiction spaceship. For $32, you can order Philippe Starck's Excalibur brush, whose hilt-like handle creates a lid when sheathed in its caddy. ... At $55, there's Stefano Giovannoni's Merdolino brush for Alessi ..."

Believe it or not, the list of options keeps going ... past the $100 mark!

shaving, the Mach3 (followed later by the Mach3Turbo) turned out to be *very* special, *very* different. And, not so incidentally, the Mach3 cost Gillette about *three-quarters of a billion dollars* to develop. (I didn't say design was a ... Free Good.)

The OralB CrossAction toothbrush ... also from Gillette ... is another Prime Time Design Example. It changed the brushing of teeth! It cost $70 million to develop. Intriguing fact: Gillette took out 23 patents on this "mere" toothbrush—including six patents for the packaging alone.

Design. About services as much as lumps. About the HR and IS departments as much as about new product development. And about $0.79 items as much as $79,000 items. Those are the Terms of Reference with which I approach this Very Big Idea.

PACKAGE MAKES PERFECT

Good things come in swell packages. Or, rather: Successful Things come in ... Great Packages.

In 1870, oatmeal was eaten by "horses and a few stray Scots." By 1890, oatmeal was an established "delicacy for the epicure, a nutritious dainty for the invalid, a delight to the children." The secret to this transformation? A humble box. More precisely, the round and still iconic Quaker Oats container.

That's the story, according to Thomas Hine in his engaging book The Total Package: The Secret History and Hidden Meanings of Boxes, Bottles, Cans, and Other Persuasive Containers. *"Packages have personality," Hine writes. "They create confidence and trust. They spark fantasies. They move the goods quickly."*

And seconds count. Hine reports that grocery consumers are aware of 30,000 items in the typical 1,800 seconds that they spend walking a store's aisles. Translation: Designers have .06 second (!) to make a ... Lasting Impression ... on the consumer.

Designing Women
And now for Something Totally Controversial ...

Men *cannot* design for *women's* needs! (Gulp.)

When I made that statement at a design conference a few years back... well, boy, did I ever stir the pot—and bring it to an instant boil!

An architect friend of mine (female) told me about a friend of hers (also female) who was shopping for a relatively pricey house. One day she looked at half a dozen properties. Only one had a laundry room on the second floor—where the kids' bedrooms were. Guess what? That house was the only one of the bunch designed by a woman.

The fact is, no guy would ever think ... not in a million years ... to put a laundry room on the second floor ... near the kids' bedrooms.

Is a second-floor laundry room a Big Deal ... worthy of an Oceanic Generalization? Of course not. But it is ... INDICATIVE. Because ... from the mundane to the profound ... from residential housing to financial services ... when it comes to designing products and services that women use, Guys Are Seriously Impaired.

STAR(C)K REALIZATION

It's a woman's world!

"Perhaps the macho look can be interesting," designer Philippe Starck writes in Harvard Design Magazine, *"if you want to fight dinosaurs. But now to survive you need intelligence, not power and aggression. Modern intelligence means intuition—it's female."*

(And for more on the "future is female" theme, see the companion volumes Essentials: Trends *and* Essentials: Leadership.*)*

Design Voices

Design is Exhibit No.1 in the "I know it when I see it" museum. We know "cool," and we know "uncool." And we don't need a detailed manual to tell one from the other. Perhaps the best way that I can define "design" is to steal some comments by others that I've come across. (The lion's share of what follows comes courtesy of the Design Council in the United Kingdom.)

"Design is about demonstrating how beautiful something can be. It has a very profound capacity. Design is a way of changing life and influencing the future."—**Sir Ernest Hall, Dean Clough**

Every new product or service that Virgin group offers must: (1) Have the best quality, (2) provide great value, (3) be innovative, (4) dramatically challenge existing alternatives, and (5) provide a "sense of fun" or "cheekiness."—**Richard Branson, CEO of Virgin Group**

"It was a revelation to discover how design could ... change people's behavior. I learnt that simply by altering the graphic content of an exhibit you could double the number of people who visited."
—**Gillian Thomas, formerly of The Science Museum/UK**

"Outstandingly good design in service industries is not an optional extra. It is an essential part of everything a company does and what it stands for."—**Richard Dykes, Managing Director, Royal Mail**

THESE KIDS ARE ALL RIGHT

Leave it to the 10- and 11-year-olds polled by UK's Design Council to "get" the essence of design from the start:

"Designers are people who think with their hearts."—James, age 10

"If there was no design there would be nothing to do, and nothing would progress or get better. The world would fall apart."—Anna, age 11

"My favourite design is the Nike 'tick' because it makes me feel confident—even though I am not so good at sports."—Raoul, age 11

"The future will fascinate. A place where experience becomes more important than information, truth more important than technology, and ideas the only global currency."—**Ralph Ardill, Imagination**

"I wish that more money and time was spent on designing an exceptional product, and less on trying to psychologically manipulate perceptions through expensive advertising campaigns."
—**Phil Kotler, marketing guru**

"Design is one of the few tools that for every [dollar] you spend, you actually say something about your business. ... You have it in your power to use design to further the wealth and prosperity of your business."
—**Raymond Turner, BAA/British Airports Authority**

"Lust for beauty and elegance UNDERPINNED the most important discoveries in computational history." ... *"The beauty of a proof or a machine lies in a happy marriage of simplicity and power."* ... *"Beauty is the ultimate defense against complexity."* ... *"A good programmer can be a hundred times more productive than an average one ... . The gap has little to do with technical or mathematical or engineering training, and much to do with taste, good JUDGMENT, aesthetic gifts."*—**David Gelernter, *Machine Beauty: Elegance and the Heart of Technology***

design

!

the "soul" of new enterprise

WORDS TO DESIGN BY

Consider the words that emerge from this chorus of "design voices":

"A way of demonstrating how beautiful something can be."

"A way of changing life and influencing the future."

"Sense of fun or cheekiness."

"Future will fascinate."

"Lust for beauty and elegance."

"The ultimate defense against complexity."

"Happy marriage of simplicity and power."

These are words and phrases that are all too seldom heard in the Sacred Halls of Business.

WHY NOT? (Damn it!)

17 Habits of Highly Successful Design-Driven Companies

Suppose you decided to make design a Top Priority at your enterprise. What would you do? Here are some ideas on how to start. *Design-Driven Companies ...*

1 Put design on the Agenda of every meeting— in Every Department throughout the Enterprise.

2 Include Professional Designers on virtually all project teams.

3 Build physical facilities that Sing and Scintillate, that reflect the SERIOUSLY COOL DESIGN SENSITIVITY of the products and services that the Enterprise produces.

4 Have internal and external Academy Awards (for employees, new products, vendors) that focus on DESIGN ... per se.

5 Measure the amount of External Recognition the enterprise gets for its design activities.

6 Put diversity front and center: The essence of Design Excellence is sensitivity to the ... Dramatically Different, often subtle needs of

WORK SPACE: THE FINAL FRONTIER

Designer Niels Diffrient, writing in a piece for *Metropolis* magazine: "My ideal office wouldn't have a chair. You would do two things there: stand up or lie down. These are probably the most natural positions the human body can take."

Designer Lise Anne Couture says: "I think it's a chicken-and-egg proposition: do furniture manufacturers make cubes because of the demand, or is the demand there because it's artificially created by the absence of any real alternatives?"

Both comments resonate with me. A few years ago, I addressed a group of corporate real estate professionals. I talked about the changing nature of work. Then I said, almost as an aside, "If you'd 'decorate' your living room with Steelcase 'furniture,' then do so with your office. If not ..."

"Work space" is important. ALL IMPORTANT.

I am disgusted by how "human-unfriendly" 99 percent of work spaces are. (Especially the ones that win awards.)

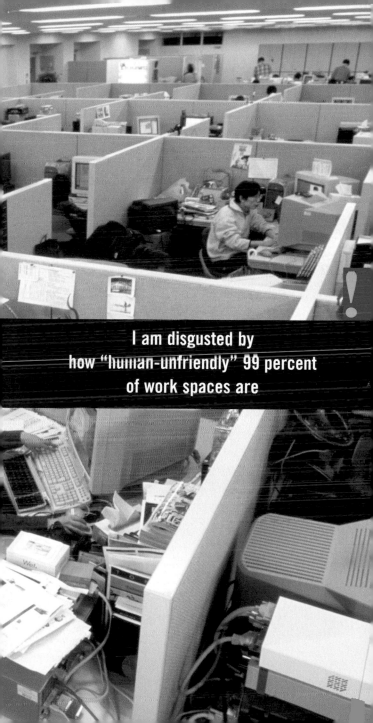

I am disgusted by
how "human-unfriendly" 99 percent
of work spaces are

various members of an organization's internal and external communities.

7 Feature Design Sensitivity explicitly in ... ALL training activities ... and in ALL performance evaluations. Universal truism: WHAT GETS MEASURED GETS DONE—and that applies to "doing" design.

8 Openly use the Emotional Language of Design. Steve Jobs, Apple founder, talks about creating "insanely great" products. Love that: *Insanely Great*. People who are Design Fanatics use such ... Hot Language. And are comfortable with it.

9 Create and authorize a posse of formal "Design Cops" (YES ... COPS!) to ... Stomp Out All Vestiges of Lousy Design—internally within departments as well as externally with regard to the business or retail consumer.

10 Have a Formal Design Board ... one that includes external as well as internal members ... that oversees the Strategic Design Sensitivity Program.

11 Talk openly about the Design Mindfulness of their "corporate culture"—and work, systematically and programmatically, to insure that it is fostered.

12 Routinely invite Top Designers to address the company as a whole. THE IDEA: KEEP THE HEAT ON—IN PERPETUITY—RELATIVE TO THE DESIGN IMPERATIVE.

13 Have a strong, formal "design function." DESIGN SHOWS UP ON THE ORGANIZATION CHART ... NEAR THE TOP.

14 The Chief Designer is a Member of the Board of Directors or, at the very least, a member of the Executive Committee. (RANK DOES MATTER.)

15 Have great art on the walls. The late Jay Chiat of Chiat/Day, for example, believed that having great art around the firm's office would inspire its teams to create Great Ads.

16 Support the arts. "Design-centric" enterprises pay attention to Community Activities that emphasize design. The message here: "DESIGN IS PART OF OUR CHARACTER."

design !

the "soul" of new enterprise

(DE)SIGN OF THE TIMES
From a July 2002 report in *BusinessWeek:* "After watching consumers flock to striking new foreign models, U.S. auto makers have been recruiting hot designers from European rivals and paying fat salaries to design-school graduates. More important, they're giving designers and marketers a stronger voice in developing new models, and they're lifting design bosses higher in the corporate hierarchy. The result: no more Sedans shaped like jelly beans. Detroit is turning out head-turners such as the retro Chrysler PT Cruiser, the Euro-styled Ford Focus, and designs that morph into a cargo hauler."

17 Have an annual or biannual ... "Design Audit" ... the results of which appear in the Annual Report. Or in a special Annual/Biannual *Design* Report.

This is a strong set of "requirements." I don't suspect any enterprise would tackle them all. The point of this "laundry list" is to suggest that this "soft," seemingly "emotional" idea of a "Design-Driven Company" can be translated into ... Hard Practical Actions.

Be Your Own Design Critic

Perhaps you're not artistic. I'm not. (Understatement.) Is there any hope? I have no doubt that there is. And I'm a case in point. I'm no more artistic than I was 30 or 40 years ago. I dropped out of architecture school and took up civil engineering, because of my total lack of artistic ability. But I can say, for certain, that I'm a great deal more "design sensitive" than I was 10 years ago.

My secret: Waking up. Becoming alert.

My trick: Creating and keeping ... a *Design Notebook*. Mine is a simple item, purchased at a Ryman's in London. On the front cover I wrote "COOL." On the back cover I wrote "CRAPPY." Then I started recording things that caught my attention. Little things mostly. Things that pissed me off. Shampoo bottles on which I couldn't read the word "Shampoo." Signage that misled me. Software commands that were silly. Those were the negatives.

design

the "soul" of new enterprise

DESIGNING MINDS

In mid-2004, I was treated to an advance copy of Dan Pink's latest book, *A Whole New Mind*. I wrote a much-deserved over-the-top blurb for it.

The book's message (in so many words): The future belongs to those with ... A Mind for Design.

Pink writes, "The last few decades have belonged to a certain kind of person with a certain kind of mind—computer programmers who could crank code, lawyers who could craft contracts, MBAs who could crunch numbers. But the keys to the kingdom are changing hands. The future belongs to a very different kind of person with a very different kind of mind— creators and empathizers, pattern recognizers and meaning makers. These people—artists, inventors, designers, storytellers, caregivers, consolers, big picture thinkers—will now reap society's richest rewards and share its greatest joys."

One other zinger that says it all: "The MFA [Master of Fine Arts] is the new MBA."

COOL

☺

_____

_____

_____

_____

_____

_____

_____

_____

CRAPPY

☹

_____

_____

_____

_____

_____

_____

_____

_____

_____

design

!

the "soul" of new enterprise

Pay especially close attention to signage

Then there were things that thrilled me. Ziplocs.
The Westin Heavenly Bed. None of these examples was
necessarily related to what I do for a living—write and
give lectures and so forth. But compiling the list made
me a lot more ... *sensitive*. Made me aware of all the
dozens upon dozens of Design Variables that are at play
... when I give a presentation ... or when I undertake the
writing of a book.

FLEX YOUR DESIGN MUSCLE

Here are some design warm-up exercises you might try:

1. Save great—and awful—junk mail. Why do you love *this one? Why
do you* hate *that one?*

*2. Take $10 and go on a shopping spree. Learn how design comes at
$2.95 ... not just at $22,295.*

*3. Pay especially close attention to signage. And instruction manuals.
(Warning: Doing so will drive you crazy—but it's well worth the effort.)*

*4. Compare the order forms or other data fields at various Web sites
that you use. (The Web, after all, is a Pure Design Medium.)*

"Design Rage": Stop Blaming Yourself!

Another design "secret," courtesy of design observer and
curmudgeon Donald Norman (author of, among other
books, *The Design of Everyday Things*):

STOP BLAMING YOURSELF.

Norman insists that one
of the Primary Problems that
we have in Paying Attention to
Design is assuming ... whenever
there is a screw-up ... that it's
because ... *we* are such klutzes.

Well, we may or may not be
"klutzes," but when you have
trouble, again and again, with
some computer program ... Blame the Dreadful Designer!
Design (Bad Design) is what causes those glitches ...
because the designer in question wasn't sensitive to
you—a normal, or perhaps novice, user of that program.

I like what reporter Susan Casey wrote a few years ago
in an online magazine piece: "I sometimes have episodes

of wild fury in rental cars. It's not road rage. It's more like design rage."

I'm not suggesting that you go out and shoot designers. (Not even the lousy ones.) I *am* suggesting that "Design Rage" is a *brilliant* starting point when it comes to raising Design Sensitivity.

Now, of course, we must translate the Design Sensitivity that we encounter in everyday life back into our own world … our own work life … our own company … our own department.

What a difference Brilliant Design can make!

What a difference Awful Design can make!

(B)SCHOOL FOR SCANDAL

Whatever you do, don't direct your Design Rage only at designers.

Other prime targets: businesses. And … business schools.

The esteemed Design Management Institute devoted the Summer 2002 issue of its journal to design and business education. One article included a survey of "design in core and elective classes" in "top business programs." Here's a selection of the results (sample sizes vary from question to question):

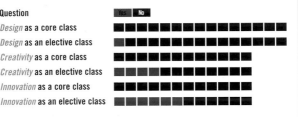

Question	Yes	No
Design as a core class		
Design as an elective class		
Creativity as a core class		
Creativity as an elective class		
Innovation as a core class		
Innovation as an elective class		

One dean's (very revealing) explanation for the lack of focus on design, creativity, and innovation at his institution: "Our programs are very quantitatively focused. It's the background of making decisions—the skills and processes to make decisions."

I guess he is content simply to train future controllers for the likes of Enron, Tyco, and WorldCom. His comment, and this survey, only make dimmer my already very dim view of Business Education As Usual.

Addendum: Maybe, instead of trying to get B-schools to teach design, we should just find a way to teach business at a … design *school. Fashion mogul Ralph Lauren, as quoted in a September 2004 article in the* International Herald Tribune: *"What I really want to do is a design school, to teach the sensibility of what goes into design, the building of a business into a company with a point of view."*

Design

=

Soul.

Believe it.

Design Voices (Redux)

More words of wisdom on design's large (and potentially enormous) place in the universe ...

DESIGNED FOR WORSHIP
"Design is treated like a religion at BMW."
—*Fortune* magazine

DESIGNED FOR DESIRE
"Every now and then, a design comes along that radically changes the way we think about a particular object. Case in point: the iMac. Suddenly, a computer is no longer an anonymous box. It is a sculpture, an object of desire, something that you look at."
—Katherine McCoy and Michael McCoy, Illinois Institute of Technology

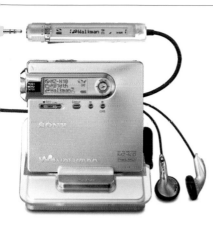

DESIGNED FOR DIFFERENCE

"At Sony we assume that all products of our competitors have basically the same technology, price, performance, and features. Design is the only thing that differentiates one product from another in the marketplace."
—Norio Ohga, retired chairman of Sony

DESIGNED FOR COMPETITION

"Fifteen years ago, companies competed on price. Today it's quality. Tomorrow it's design."
—Bob Hayes, professor emeritus at the Harvard Business School

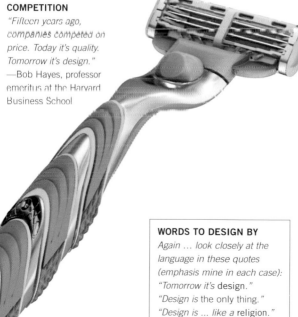

WORDS TO DESIGN BY

Again ... look closely at the language in these quotes (emphasis mine in each case):
"Tomorrow it's design.*"*
"Design is the only thing.*"*
"Design is ... like a religion.*"*
"Object of desire.*"*

design

the "soul" of new enterprise

Object of Design

Billions upon billions of dollars are at stake. (Trillions?) Some companies do get it: Sony. Nike. Gillette. Apple. Body Shop. VW. Amazon. Nokia. Target. Bloomberg.

Nothing ... NOTHING ... (!!!) ...

is more important to the executives of these enterprises than unabashed ... *Fanaticism* ... about ... *Design.*

But most companies (the vast majority!) don't get it. Hence they don't really bother about design. (And it *is* a bother. It's damned hard work, and it requires constant care and attention and love and affection and ... obsession.) And those that don't bother are, to put it simply ... BLOWING OFF A V-E-R-Y BIG THING.

That language is strong.

That language is emotional.

But that language is also ... an expression of *frustration.* Frustration caused by the widespread failure to "get" what Steve Jobs (for example) so obviously gets. Jobs got it *exactly* right when he said, "Design is the fundamental soul of a man-made creation." You don't become "design-minded" by opening a checkbook, spending a few hundred thousand dollars on a "great designer"—and then telling him/her to please "do the 'design thing.'"

Design is soul deep. And so important.

Design = Soul.

Believe it.

DESIGN STARTS AT HOME
Re-imagine! Business Excellence in a Disruptive Age (2003)—the big book that inspired the little book that you hold in your hand—marked a startling departure from my previous literary efforts.

New publisher.

New theory of the case.

New ... DESIGN.

My decision to throw in my hat with Dorling Kindersley came at the urging of my wife, an artist and designer who loved DK's books because of their fabulous design. Also, it turned out that the DK leadership team and I shared an ambition that is very close to my heart. To reinvent the

Business Book. To make it as energetic as business itself can be at its best.

And, yes, to create a Business Book that is design-driven.

The same goes for this book on ... Design!

(Sidebar, vertical text): design ! the "soul" of new enterprise

TOP 10 TO-DOs

1. *Be a "Soul" supplier.* At every point in your Design process, do a soul-check on what you are creating. In other words: Don't think *Pretty*. Think *Profound*.

2. *List your "loves."* Get a little notebook, or open a file on your computer, and keep track of product and service offerings that earn your ... Enduring Ardor.

3. *Harness your "hates."* While you're at it, keep track of stuff that earns your ... Absolute Enmity. Think about the common attributes of the stuff on both sides of the ledger.

4. *If it feels good, dote on it.* Cultivate a fingertip feel for Design-induced Emotional Attachment. Find a way to carry "it" around with you ... just as I carry around my turnbuckle!

5. *Be of service.* Foster a Design-driven approach to the way that you develop not just lumps of stuff ... but also service offerings and business processes. (That means you, Finance Department Head!)

6. *Hunt for bargains.* Look inside your medicine cabinet, your toolbox, your kitchen cabinet. Learn from items therein that are low in cost and high in Design Impact.

7. *Judge everything by its cover.* Make every package worthy of its product. Just because Design is not a surface thing (per se) doesn't mean that surfaces don't matter.

8. *Watch for signs.* Monitor the signage all around you for examples of Soulful Direction and Woeful Misdirection.

9. *Be true to forms.* Invest time, energy, and Design Know-How in the creation of all (ALL) business documents.

10. *Rage on.* Get mad, and get even—with companies that offer shoddily designed stuff. Remember: It's their fault, not yours.

COOL FRIEND: Virginia Postrel

Virginia Postrel writes an economics column for the New York Times *and is the author of* The Future and Its Enemies: The Growing Conflict Over Creativity, Enterprise, and Progress *(1998). Below are some remarks she made on the occasion of publishing her recent (highly Design-Driven) book,* The Substance of Style: How the Rise of Aesthetic Value is Remaking Commerce, Culture, and Consciousness *(2003).*

I write about toilet brushes for two reasons. First, because it is an example of something purely functional that has over the last five to ten years become a designed object, designed for aesthetic pleasure. And, second, because you don't use a toilet brush to impress the neighbors. It's not a status symbol. This is aesthetics for pleasure and ... personal meaning, not for status competition.

* *

What's going on ... is that we see large percentage increases in prices that are very small dollar amount increases. You're talking about going from a $4 brush to a $12 brush. That's a 200 percent increase, but the total is still only 12 dollars. It's a relatively inexpensive way to incorporate a little more aesthetic pleasure into your life. ... If you observe people when you're out shopping, you hear a lot of "this is so cool," or "isn't that cute," or "isn't that pretty." It's that immediate reaction, particularly when we're dealing with these kinds of goods that are not luxury goods.

* *

For 100 years or so people obviously didn't lose their appreciation of aesthetics, but given relative prices and economic progress, what suddenly was impressive and available was not so much the look and feel, the sensory content of these goods and services, it was having these goods or services at all. Yes, in some cases, the automobile for an obvious example, there were periods when there was a lot of attention to aesthetics. At other points characteristics such as functionality and convenience were more important. When automobiles matured as an industry in the '50s and '60s, aesthetics became very important. Then in the '70s and '80s the combination of concerns about the energy and efficiency and the competition on the basis of reliability among the manufacturers made the other dimensions more important. Now, quality is very high and prices are competitive, so people are looking for more aesthetics in their cars, more personal definition.

There was a period where mass manufacturing, mass distribution, was the great form of economic progress. And it was progress, compared to what had gone before. But when you're making things in mass quantities, what you have to do is design to the lowest common denominator of aesthetics because if the aesthetic content is too intense, if the design is too strong, you inevitably please some people and alienate others.

What we have now for a variety of reasons is the ability to produce and deliver more variety. And, as a result, when you can offer more variety, you can also offer more intensity because you can please some people and alienate others with this design, but over here you have this other design to please a different group of people, and alienate the people who liked the first one.

* *

Part of what we see today is a ratchet effect. As people are exposed to designed public spaces, they come to expect this same kind of aesthetic treatment everywhere. For example, in the '50s, if you went out to a restaurant outside of the largest cities, it probably was chosen essentially to get the same food that you would have had at home. The point of going out was to save Mom from having to cook and then clean up afterwards. The restaurant's atmosphere was nothing to write home about, and the food wasn't even all that exciting. But it served its purpose and people were happy to have it. Eating out was still a kind of luxury, and you didn't do it a lot.

Today that would not wash, except perhaps in some nostalgic sense of "Oh, this is what we used to do when I was a kid." Now people expect to have better food, different cuisines, and certainly a much more designed environment. You don't have to go all the way back to the '50s cafeteria-style restaurants to get that contrast. Just look at the contrast between Pizza Hut, which was a standard suburban pizza restaurant in the '70s, versus California Pizza Kitchen, which is also standard now and found throughout suburban America. There's a huge contrast in the total aesthetics of the experience, from the food itself to the look and feel of the restaurant.

* *

[W]hatever we choose to do aesthetically, including the choice to ignore aesthetics, will be interpreted by others as a way of saying something about who we are. ...

I talk about Hillary Clinton's hair and the way people interpreted it, and the jokes she's made about it. She's quoted as saying, "The most important thing I've learned is to pay attention to your hair because everybody else will." Here was a woman who hadn't paid attention to her hair and how people might interpret it, and suddenly there she was in the public eye. She didn't have her own personal style. Whether people liked her or disliked her, they read into her changing hair styles meanings that might have been there or might not have been there. Because she hadn't defined her own aesthetic, she wasn't controlling the discussion.

The same thing is true for business. If you're running a restaurant, how you design the atmosphere will say something to your customers about who you expect them to be, about who you are. If you don't do anything, if you just keep the building the way it was when you inherited it, or you put together a hodge-podge, whatever's convenient, that will say something else.

* *

This is a double-edged sword. As consumers, as people buying things in the marketplace, or just people walking down the street, looking at the environment, looking at other people, this is all wonderful, because it results in a more beautiful, more interesting, more stimulating, better-designed world. That's great.

However, as producers, whether that's business producers or just people deciding how to get dressed in the morning, it puts more pressure on us and is another form of competition. It's not as simple as that vertical status competition where if I spend more money I'll be higher on the totem pole. It's actually a harder form of competition than that traditional "keeping up with the Joneses" competition. Because it's about paying attention, it's about thinking about how to match your outside and your inside or your identity and your aesthetic, whether that's personal or organizational or whatever that might be.

* *

[T]hink about the design of places. ... [R]estaurants, stores like Starbucks, and public noncommercial places like libraries, churches, airports are paying much more attention to ... the aesthetic, to the lighting, to the floor coverings, the textures of the furniture—to creating an aesthetic environment in which people want to spend time. In a sense the organization brings the pleasure, that value of aesthetics, and the customers bring the meaning, the other value. They spend time in a successful place. Again, Starbucks is the touchstone, but not the only example. Customers have experiences there, and it becomes meaningful to them as a social space.

* *

The guy who is making granite countertops for the bathroom in your house is part of this aesthetic economy, and all these kinds of craft professions are growth areas. But he's not creating an experience, he's helping create an environment in which you, the consumer, will create your own experiences because it's your house.

* *

This aesthetic definition of identity always has two components: I like that. I'm like that. This is me, what I like, and who else I associate myself with.

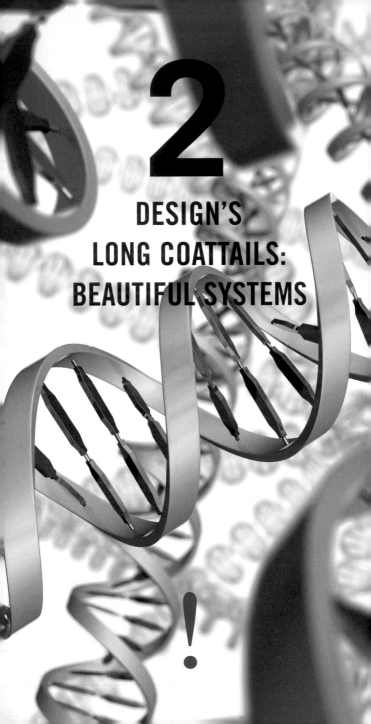

2

DESIGN'S
LONG COATTAILS:
BEAUTIFUL SYSTEMS

Contrasts

Was	Is
More	Less
Efficient	Elegant
Off-putting	Welcoming
Slapped together	Organically whole
Impedes communication	Spurs communication
Closed	Open
"Let the techies handle it"	"Bring in design-driven leaders"
Complex	Simple
Obscure	Clear
Awkward	Graceful
Ugly	Beautiful

!Rant

We are not prepared ...

We avoid words like "beauty"—and **THE CONCEPT OF BEAUTY**—between 9 a.m. and 5 p.m. (Especially if we work in a department like HR or IS or Logistics.) • But as part of the urgent process of re-imagining enterprise, we must embrace both the word and the concept—and **MAKE BEAUTY THE PRIMARY ATTRIBUTE NOT ONLY OF PRODUCT DESIGN BUT ALSO OF PROCESS DESIGN.** • In short, we must create a business environment in which **enterprise systems become nothing less than ... Beautiful Systems.**

!Vision

I imagine ...

A Policy Manual ... in HR or IS or Logistics ... **THAT IS ONE PAGE LONG.**

A hospital's patient consent form or a title insurance policy that is **WRITTEN IN ... PLAIN ENGLISH.**

A plane that flies directly from someplace I'm leaving to someplace I'm going ... without a long layover in a "hub."

A Web site where I can COMPLETE A TRANSACTION ... IN 90 SECONDS.

design

Beauty ...

The Napkin: Today, you'll find a replica of it on a wall at company headquarters in Dallas. (Quite possibly, for the sake of veracity, it's stained with Wild Turkey—the founder's favorite.) On the original napkin, which Herb Kelleher and colleague Rollin King sketched out at a bar in San Antonio in 1966, you'll observe a simple triangle. At the three corners you'll find ... San Antonio ... Houston ... Dallas. And from that *beautiful* triangle has emerged nothing less than Earth's Best Airline. Namely, of course, Southwest.

The absolute, gorgeous simplicity that marked that original sketch-route design has subsequently been applied to every activity that Southwest undertakes. The airline's exceptionally low cost structure is a direct reflection of the approach set forth on that napkin.

Herb's napkin was ... beautiful.
And Southwest Airlines is a ... beautiful system.

beautiful systems

The Thesis: The paper got a C grade. In 1965, the idea outlined therein seemed silly: You're in a hurry to send a package from Manhattan to Newark. Gotta get it there. Absolutely, positively gotta get it there. The obvious solution: Send it via Memphis! In that thesis, which barely earned passing marks for Fred Smith at Yale, lay the origins of Smith's hub-and-spoke concept—a concept

GRACE NOTE

Another word for "beauty" (and a key word in my lexicon) is ... "grace."

Designer Celeste Cooper gets right to the point: "My favorite word is 'grace'—whether it's 'amazing grace,' 'saving grace,' 'grace under fire,' Grace Kelly. How we live contributes to beauty—whether it's how we treat other people or the environment."

Yes, I've fallen madly in love with ... 'grace.' And it's led me to wonder: Why so little discussion of 'grace' in management books, or in the hallways and conference rooms of enterprise?

that changed package delivery. Indeed, the company that grew out of his thesis has changed life itself, for a lot of us. Namely, of course, Federal Express.

Fred's thesis was ... beautiful. And Federal Express is a ... beautiful system.

design

TAKE A DEEP BREATH

Please consider this ... Beautiful Syllogism:

Is the respiratory system central to the body? Of course!

Is an "organizational system" to business what the respiratory system is to the body? Of course!

Is the respiratory system worth "getting worked up about"? Of course!

Is an organizational system worth "getting worked up about"? Of course!

---

beautiful systems

... And the Beast

I'm willing to bet a pretty penny that when the talk turns to "systems," one seldom hears terms such as "beauty," "aesthetic virtue," "grace," and a dozen other words of that sort.

When we think about "systems" or "processes" we think about nuts and bolts—the dirty engineering details—that go into creating something that will "get the job done." With some efficiency.

And yet most of the trouble businesses get into—in serving their customers and in general getting things done with dispatch—is directly attributable to the *ugliness* of their systems and processes.

Over time, even a beautiful system tends to get elaborated and elaborated ... and then more elaborated ... with every change. Each one made, of course, for a "good reason." Until the whole ugly, sloppy, inefficient, demoralizing, dehumanizing mess makes everybody unhappy. We end up "serving the system" rather than having the system serve us.

The *Real* Obesity Epidemic

Think "systems," and ordinarily what comes to mind is Obese Manuals ... thousands of pages of fine print ... lining the walls of every department in every organization, public or private. Or Obese Files ... paper or electronic ... adding up to thousands upon thousands of reasons not to act ... or to delay action ... on any and every initiative.

LIVING OFF THE FAT OF THE LAW

The accounting debacles that humbled business in 2002 (and beyond) owed a great deal to the gradual larding-up of rules and regulations.

Here's legendary Citicorp chairman Walter Wriston, writing in a Wall Street Journal article titled "The Solution to Scandals? Simpler Rules:"

"The Financial Accounting Standards Board has, at last count, enshrined generally accepted accounting principles into three volumes comprising some 4,530 pages. Some of the FASB rules run to over 700 pages on how to book a single transaction. It should surprise no one that two skilled accountants, looking at the booking of the same transaction and using their knowledge of the same rules, come out with different results.

"Many years ago, James Madison foresaw the problem and wrote in 'The Federalist Papers': 'It will be of little avail to the people, that the laws are made by men of their own choice, if the laws be so voluminous that they cannot be read, or so incoherent that they cannot be understood ... that no man, who knows what the law is today, can guess what it will be tomorrow.' It can be argued that we have now arrived at that point in the accounting profession."

---

design

!

beautiful systems

Obese Systems are Enemy No.1 of Change and Agility ... and Ally No.1 of the upstart commercial competitor. Hence we must not shy away from addressing "dreary" systems issues. We must understand their strategic significance and confront them squarely if change—nay, revolution—is our goal. And I believe that the best way to confront them is through a lens called "design" ... which is to say, through a lens called "beauty."

BRAND = SYSTEM
I once heard Jesper Kunde, the Danish marketing star, argue that all systems must be clearly and unequivocally "brand-driven." Every HR director, for example, should ask: Are my processes and policies ... Aesthetically Aligned ... with the Corporate Brand Promise?

That is a stunning insight. For more on Branding, see Chapter 5: "Design at the Summit: The Heart of Branding."

Obese Systems are Enemy No.1
of Change and Agility

More Than Skin-Deep

"Design," I argued in the previous chapter, goes far beyond the beauty of (say) an iMAC. Or the compelling nature of Target's logo—or the compellingly designed items found in its stores. (Though, at both Apple and Target, design fanaticism *per se* has been worth billions of dollars in market capitalization.)

One arena where design matters most—and is least considered—is in the creation of essential enterprise systems. Indeed, systems of all sorts.

One way to talk about this issue would be to say that "design" involves how a thing looks, and that "system" pertains to how a thing works. But that misses the point, which is that "design thinking" and "systems thinking" are one and the same. Or should be. In great design, form and function come together in a way that appears seamless, and every part contributes to the whole in a way that seems … inevitable. So, too, in a great system.

Hence this term that I've coined: *Beautiful Systems*.

BEAUTIFUL THOUGHT

Does "Beautiful Systems" seem like an oxymoron? It is, according to an old way of thinking. But the way we think is changing.

Here's Virginia Postrel, writing in her 2003 book, The Substance of Style: How the Rise of Aesthetic Value Is Remaking Commerce, Culture, and Consciousness: *"If modernist design ideology promised efficiency, rationality, and truth, today's diverse aesthetics offer a different trifecta: freedom, beauty, and pleasure."*

Monster Mash

Years ago, when I was a McKinsey consultant, a colleague and I developed what we called an "anthropological systems analysis."

Systems are typically invented when problems arise. Example: There's a screw-up with a customer's order. Jane Doe, head of Customer Service, devises a "system" to make sure it doesn't happen again. Great! Smart! After three years Jane is promoted and followed by Arthur Doe (no relation). During Arthur's watch, another Bad Problem quickly crops up.

What does Art do? He adds "stuff" to Jane's system. You can guess the rest of the story: Arthur Doe is succeeded by Cathy Doe (no relation), who is followed by Miriam Doe (no relation), who is followed by Richard Doe (no relation).

Each of the Assiduous Does puts his or her Stamp on the System. And, before you can say "John Doe," the system gets so elaborated that it (1) requires an army of other Does to administer and (2) leaves no room whatsoever for front-line initiative.

The Does, all well-intentioned ("Fiximus Problemi Daminatus," or "Fix the Damn Problem," is on the ancient family shield), have inadvertently created a monster. A *complex* monster. An *ugly* monster. An ugly *system*. A system that saps enterprise vitality and turns front-line operatives into anonymous Does.

design

beautiful systems

K.I.S.S. and Tell

"Beautiful systems" are simple. Allow me to illustrate that "simple" point with a story:

A book came to me with a note asking for a blurb of endorsement. I tossed it aside. (Alas, I often do that.) But it happened that my wife was in the process of starting a business. And she wanted to put together a compelling business plan.

OBSTRUCTION MANAGEMENT

Long ago, and with typical sage wisdom, Peter Drucker said, "Much of what we call management consists of making it difficult for people to get their work done."

My take: The primary reason we've "made it so damnably difficult for people to get things done" is ... *ugly systems.*

VOTE OF INCOMPETENCE

Lest you think that document design is of little moment, think back to the U.S. presidential election of 2000. Thanks to the "system" in use in Palm Beach County, Florida, thousands of voters ended up marking their ballot for the wrong guy. That poorly designed "butterfly ballot" may have cost Al Gore the White House.

Remember: A form is never *just* a form.

If you start talking about "beauty"—obsessing on "beauty"—then "beauty" will become a commonplace part of your everyday affairs! So, too, grace. So, too, clarity. So, too, simplicity.

I vaguely remembered the book. Author: Jim Horan. Title: *The One Page Business Plan*. What a silly idea, the engineer-MBA within me thought. What an interesting idea, the design freak within me thought.

So I took a look. And became fascinated. On a single page, Mr. Horan claimed, a business plan writer should be able to travel all the way from an over-arching vision to the tactical details of execution.

Again: A silly idea at face value. (Silly, just like Fred Smith's "silly" thesis.)

But, what the hell, why not give it a try?

Trust me: Mr. Horan was the devil's consultant. Putting together a *70-page* business plan—replete with the most complicated charts and graphs and spreadsheets known to humankind—is a walk in the park. Getting it all right—*exactly right*—on a single page.

Whoa!

My wife labored and labored ... and labored some more. Days and days went by. And I'm here to testify: It was *damn well worth it!* The results were ... *beautiful*.

That Jim Horan's *idea* (a one-page business plan!) is beautiful, too.

It's never too late to learn (or relearn) that old bit of sales-and-marketing wisdom: "Keep it simple, stupid." Or K.I.S.S., for short.

design !
beautiful systems

TALK ABOUT "BRIEF"!
A little dirty laundry ...

John De Laney is a counsel at International Creative Management, the agency that handled negotiations on the contract for my book *Re-imagine!* At one point in that process, I got enormously frustrated, and so I said to my agent,

"What's going on here?"

About an hour later, I got a one-third-page email from John, outlining in Plain English the serious issues. As we progressed, I received more communications from him—none of them longer than one-third of a page.

I've worked with a host of lawyers over the

years. Trust me, boiling *up* is their hallmark. John was the first Lawyer-as-Boiler-Way-Down I've ever dealt with.

Hence the Law of John De Laney: Anything Truly Important Can Be Summarized and Clarified in One-Third of a Page.

design

beautiful systems

System Overload

The magnitude of potential simplification throughout
enterprise is ... *staggering*.

Jim Champy, co-author along with Michael Hammer
of the bible on reengineering (titled *Reengineering the
Corporation*), keeps executive audiences enthralled as
he recounts tale after tale after horrid tale of critical
business processes that have gone to flab. Consider a
process at one insurance company for verifying a claim.
It took *23 working days*. Yet when Champy looked inside
the company with an electron microscope, he discovered
that only *17 minutes* of actual work were performed.
The rest was all about scraps of paper flying (or, rather,
"crawling") from here to there.
Sitting on desks. Waiting to be
initialed. And initialed some
more. And so on.

Yes, it is that bad.

23 days.

17 minutes.

Another case in point: the
pharmaceutical industry. The
requirements for patient safety
that are placed upon it are
appropriately stringent. Of that
I have no doubt. On the other
hand, the "systems" for drug
discovery that giant pharma has
created are ... well ... wildly over
the top. That is: convoluted,
sluggish, actually absurd.

> **BIG PHARMA'S
> LITTLE HELPER**
>
> *For some time now, the
> trend in Giant Pharma
> World has been to create
> alliances with smaller
> biotech companies.*
>
> *Why? Simple: Big
> Pharma is seeking a way
> around its own ungainly
> systems. The biotech
> companies attract more
> interesting talent, to
> be sure. But, far more
> important, they haven't
> had time to develop
> systems that are so
> elaborated that they make
> it virtually impossible to
> get anything done!*

Too Many ~~Cooks~~ Engineers

Gordon Bell is the developer, of among many other things,
the fabled VAX operating system that revolutionized the
minicomputer industry at Digital Equipment. Several years
ago, after one of his presentations, Gordon and I chatted.
He waxed particularly eloquent about this simplicity
business—and about bureaucracies run amok. "I've never

seen a project being worked on by 500 engineers," Bell flatly stated, "that couldn't be done better by 50."

Think about that statement. The idea here is not to introduce a "touch of efficiency"—and shave a 500-person engineering team to 462. (No small saving!) No, the idea here is a 90 percent cut ... from 500 to 50.

Charles Wang, the crusty and brilliant founder of Computer Associates, has always been the software industry's resident contrarian. He and Bell emerged, it would appear, from the same peapod. The Word According to Wang: If a project team is behind schedule, what do you do—double the assets (people)? No, no, no. You do the opposite. You identify the least productive 25 percent of the folks on that team ... and eliminate them!

Wang Rule: No job being done sloppily and slowly by 30 people can't be done better by the Best 23 of those people. (Gordon Bell might well say "the Best 3.")

> **Systems. Must have. Must HATE.**

design

beautiful systems

GAMING THE SYSTEM

*Years ago, Wal*Mart introduced an employee contest, replete with awards and prizes of all sorts. The idea was that everyone in the company should identify the "stupidest thing we do around here."*

Frankly, I think that's a lot better than a "suggestion" system. Suggestion systems usually end up adding more (useless) stuff. Instead, this program focused on subtraction.

Addition is the exercise of fools. Subtraction is the exercise of genius.

(Not a new idea. The greatest sculptors have hewed to the same path. How do you do a brilliant sculpture of X? You take a gorgeous piece of stone and simply remove everything that's not X.)

Systems: Can't Live With 'Em, Can't Live Without 'Em

I am *not* an anarchist.

The world is a complicated place. Damn complicated if you're managing General Electric or ExxonMobil. And pretty damn complicated if you're running a 26-table Mexican restaurant in El Paso, Texas.

BEAUTIFUL SYSTEM: BEEN THERE, DUNG THAT

Garth Thompson, the guide who took my family and me on safari in Zimbabwe in 2001, is one of the world's leading experts on elephants. Through his tutelage I came to revere those extraordinary creatures. Yet it was the ... termites ... that mesmerized me. These talented creatures routinely build mounds that are 20 or 30 feet high. (That's about 3,000 times the termite's height; the tallest man-made structure is about 300 times our height. Talk about excellence in structural engineering!)

But here's what really got me in a tizzy:

Elephants have inefficient digestive systems. What is perhaps bad news for the elephant is good news for the termite. As a result of such digestive failure, elephant dung is loaded with nutritious goodies. And that's where the story really gets interesting.

Let's say a termite construction site—a termite mound-to-be—is 200 yards from an elephant watering hole, where dung is plentiful. The termites' "GPS" (global positioning system) somehow locks on to the dung warehouse, and the creatures then launch a precision-guided underground assault. But they don't leave the mound empty-mouthed; each termite lugs a monstrously large grain or two of sand or soil. Soon these raiders pop up under the dung treasure site and extract succulent morsels that the elephant had grabbed from a tree 25 feet above ground. In place of the extracted food parcel, the termites deposit their grains of soil or sand.

I go to the watering hole and am awestruck by the Termite Skyscraper. Then Garth Thompson orders me to pick up an old piece of elephant "dung." I reluctantly do so—it damn well looks like shit to me—and I'm in for a shock.

The "dung" turns out to be 100 percent sand or soil!

Yes, I was mesmerized. And, ever unable to put my passion for management aside, I said to no one in particular, "Now, there is a ... Truly Beautiful System." Beauty ... Clarity ... Grace ... Efficiency ... Elegance ... all-in-one. Now if only our enterprise systems could match such design excellence!

Thus, we must have systems.

Must have them. Period.

But just as we must have them, so also must we hate them. *Must hate them.* Period

Systems: Must have. Must hate.

Systems: Must design. Must un-design.

That's *the* secret.

There's another secret. The Big One: There are no "bad guys (or gals)" here. The Road to Systems Hell is truly paved with Good Intentions. (Remember those ubiquitous well-intended Does.)

Help Wanted: EVP (SOUB)

The only answer to The Big Systems Conundrum: MAKE PERPETUAL WAR ON THE VERY (LIFE-SUSTAINING) SYSTEMS THAT WE HAVE CREATED.

I once worked with the management team at a growth company that was trying (desperately) to stay "entrepreneurial." Trying (desperately) to acknowledge the complexities that attend growth. The upshot of our labors was to add an executive position with an intriguing name. (Their idea, not mine.)

Said name: EVP/SOUB.

Figure it out yet? It stands for ... *Executive Vice President/Stomping Out Unnecessary Bullshit.*

I am not flipping off the real world. I want a brilliant systems designer sitting in Room 103. And right across the hall, in Room 104, I want his equally powerful peer, the *de facto* or *de jure* EVP/SOUB. I want the guy in Room 103 to work 19 hours a day to deal with problems, to get the systems "right." And I want the gal in Room 104 to work 19.1 hours a day to unwind the whole damn, stultifying thing ... just as it's being built!

CHAPTER AND VERSE

Poets. Poets. Poets.

That's the meta-message of this chapter: We need fewer techies and more poets in our systems design shop. And more artists ... and more jazz musicians ... and more dancers ... You get the idea. (I hope!)

Beauty Contest

I pray that this brief screed has introduced you to the idea of ... BEAUTIFUL SYSTEMS. Now I'd like to extend this idea with ... a Beauty Contest! Here's how it works:

1. Select a single form or document in use at your company: invoice, airbill, sick leave policy, customer returns claim form.

2. Rate the selected document on a scale of 1 to 10 on four dimensions [1 = Pitiful; 10 = Work of Art]:

design

beautiful systems

SIMPLICITY. ☐

CLARITY. ☐

GRACE. ☐

BEAUTY. ☐

3. Reinvent the document in the next 15 working days. Re-assess, using the criteria in Step 2.

4. Repeat, with another form or document, once per month. Forever.

Why shouldn't an invoice be a ... Work of Art? (After all, it's an important point-of-contact/moment-of-truth with a customer!) Why shouldn't a sick-leave policy be a Work of Art?

(Given the importance of attracting the Best Talent, one would hope that an HR Manual would be as compelling in its presentation as a fabulous novel, albeit slightly less fictional.)

Four words: Simplicity. Clarity. Grace. Beauty.

Shouldn't any and all financial documents—any and all policy documents—be judged by that set of criteria? Shouldn't any and all company documents be ... simple ... clear ... graceful ... beautiful?

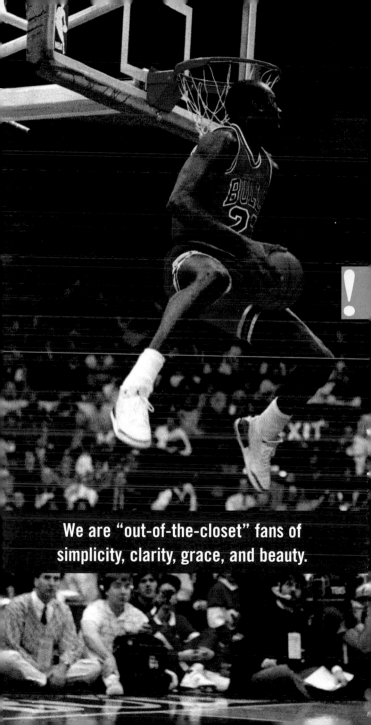

We are "out-of-the-closet" fans of simplicity, clarity, grace, and beauty.

Final Word: All Systems Go

As I see it, enterprise is all too short on *simplicity*, *clarity*, *grace*, and *beauty*.

And the near-absence of those traits flows more or less directly from the near-absence of those words from the language of business.

Here's the lesson I've learned: If you start talking about "beauty"—obsessing on "beauty"—then "beauty" will become a commonplace part of your everyday affairs! So, too, grace. So, too, clarity. So, too, simplicity.

In our "real lives" (as opposed to our "business lives"), we are "out-of-the-closet" fans of simplicity, clarity, grace, and beauty. In any work of art. In a Michael Jordan dance down the basketball court. Whatever.

So why not apply the very same criteria to a purchasing procedure? A training course? A recruiting process? An evaluation scheme? And so on. (And so on.) (And so on.)

Systems ...

Love 'em.
Hate 'em.
Design 'em.
Un-design 'em.
Make 'em simple.
Make 'em clear.
Make 'em graceful.
Make 'em beautiful.

design

beautiful systems

SYSTEMS: A SUMMARY
Here, in terms simple and clear (and graceful? ... and beautiful?), is the gist of this chapter:

Systems matter.

Systems always grow (in the main unintentionally) like Topsy.

Systems, however well-intentioned, will eventually impede innovation and thwart progress.

Systems are too important to be left to "systems administrators."

Systems must be the concern of CEOs.

Systems can ... FOSTER CHANGE.

Systems can ... FOSTER INNOVATION.

Systems can ... BE SIMPLE.

Systems can ... BE CLEAR.

Systems can ... BE GRACEFUL.

Systems can ... BE BEAUTIFUL.

TOP 10 TO-DOs

1. *Think (and rethink) "beauty."* Consider the dullest, homeliest process or system within your company, and ask: How can I make it *beautiful?*

2. *Get lean (and mean it).* Put your company, starting with its document-management system, on a reducing program. Mantra: Reduce steps and (where necessary) reduce staff.

3. *Keep it simple.* Scrutinize your every business practice for well-intentioned but (ultimately) ill-advised accretions of Bureaucratic Gunk. Remove same. Rinse. Repeat.

4. *Keep it to one page.* Distill every memo to a single page. If it's worth writing, it's worth editing.

5. *Get creative.* Call in the poets, the painters, the pianists. Call in those trained in art—in the creation of noble form and organic wholeness. (Yes, this is a *business* imperative.)

6. *Bring in relief.* Hire and empower an EVP/SOUB — Executive Vice President, Stomping Out Unnecessary Bullshit. (Okay, give him/her another title if you must ...)

7. *Take it away.* Post a "subtraction box" at your company ... in lieu of a suggestion box. (A Wal*Mart-approved idea. Enough said.)

8. *Say "Grace."* Learn to use terms like "elegance" and "grace." ("Great spreadsheet. How can we make it more graceful?")

9. *Loathe systems.* Treat every enterprise system, every established procedure, as guilty until proven innocent. If it's not *simple, clear, graceful, beautiful* ... then scrap it.

10. *Love systems.* Aspire at all times to wrest Order from Chaos. (I am not—I repeat, *not*—an anarchist.) Business is about systems. Successful business is about *Designing Beautiful Systems.*

3

DESIGN IN ACTION: PROVIDING MEMORABLE EXPERIENCES

Contrasts

Was	Is
"Product" or "Service"	"Experience"
It's good stuff	It's a kick, a hoot
It works for the moment	It leaves an indelible memory
"I'm glad I bought it"	"I want more!"
Satisfied customer	Member of a club
Repeat customer	Viral marketing agent
You get what you pay for	You get thrown for a loop
Agrees with your wallet	Agrees with your psyche
Deals with ... one of your needs	Helps define ... Who You Are

!Rant

We are not prepared ...

We still applaud the ideal of the "satisfied customer." • Instead we must **FOCUS ON CREATING A SCINTILLATING ... ENCOMPASSING ... DRAMATIC ... NOVEL ... "CUSTOMER EXPERIENCE."**

We continue to talk about **"service" and "quality" as the key attributes of Value Added** • Instead we must understand that **"EXPERIENCE" IS NOT ONLY A VERY BIG WORD** ... with far-reaching implications ... but it is nothing short of **THE BASIS FOR A ... TOTALLY RE-IMAGINED ORGANIZATIONAL LIFE FORM.** • (Truly.)

!Vision

I imagine ...

An accounting firm that provides a full-blown accounting ... **EXPERIENCE**. • **Not a "service," but rather a ... show.** • A Theater of Accounting Excellence. Yes, the tax advice is fine; the green-eyeshade stuff is all up to snuff. • **BUT IT'S THE THEATER PART THAT CLIENTS REALLY BUY ... THE CHARACTER OF THE RELATIONSHIP. • THE PROMISE OF TRANSFORMATIVE INTERACTION.**

A world in which **creating a well-designed Experience is the Beginning and End of Value Added.** • Not just at Disney World. • **NOT JUST AT STARBUCKS.** • Not just at Club Med. • But in every kind of company and **for every kind of professional** ... from fur trapping to high finance.

The Language of ... Experience

What happens when you take a well-designed Beautiful System and turn it inside-out? In other words: What is the ultimate upshot ... not for people inside the company, but for customers ... of Beautiful Systems? For customers of Great Design?

Answer: *a Full-Fledged, Memorable Experience.* Increasingly, the "value added" that a company offers ... the "stuff" that can add Billions of Dollars to its market cap ... comes from the ... Quality of the Customer Experience.

Moving Up the Value Chain has always meant ... Something More. It has meant emphasizing the ... Soft Attributes (the INTANGIBLES) ... of "Products" or "Services." Attributes such as Convenience, Comfort, Warmth, Companionship, Beauty, Trust, and ... Being Seriously Cool.

In a Word ... a word that sums up what customers get from all of those attributes ... it has meant *experience.*

BANK ON IT

Take the example of "financial services." If the price of a loan were the only issue, we'd simply go to the cheapest source. But as a small businessman, I am mostly interested in the character and depth and stability of the "relationship" with my financial service provider. Will he or she call the loan the minute I hiccup? Or will she or he make the effort to get to know me—and to become my "trusted partner"?

Believe me, if my banker becomes my "trusted partner," she'll get a Triple-A rating from me!

The Main Event

One could easily write this entire chapter off as being based on a mere "semantic twist"—the replacement of the word "service" with the word "experience." Any service offering *is* an "experience." I wouldn't deny that for a second. But words are funny things.

They can change everything.

When I think of a "service transaction," my mind is not in the same place as when I think of a trip to Disneyland, or Walt Disney World, or Circus Circus on the strip in Las Vegas, or Super Bowl Week, or the legendary

Bass Outdoor World store in Springfield, Missou[...] whole different "thing" is conjured up when a Disney (or Circus Circus, or Super Bowl, or Bass) ... *experience* ... is under consideration.

I think that difference is critical. And I think it plays directly into the Grand Vision of "Design" and "Beautiful Systems" that we explored in the previous two chapters.

For me, at least, an "experience" is far more *holistic, total, encompassing, emotional,* and *transforming* than a mere "service." A service is a *transaction.* (Good or bad.) An experience is an *Event* ... an *Adventure* ... a *Happening* ... a Soul-Jogging, Spirit-Lifting *Phenomenon.* With a beginning ... a middle ... and an end. An experience leaves an Indelible Memory (caps required), adds to my History (caps required), provides fodder for a thousand future Conversations with Old Pals and Grandkids (caps required).

Thus we have two conceptions, as different as day and night, of what a company's "offering" does.

Conception I: It pays for itself (Service).

Conception II: It makes the world wobble on its axis a bit (Experience).

To the best of my knowledge, Joe Pine and Jim Gilmore are the inventors of this idea, at least in the modern business context. Their book, *The Experience Economy: Work Is Theatre and Every Business a Stage,* is simply brilliant. Their basic hypothesis is easy to state: "Experiences," they write, "are as distinct from services as services are from goods."

"SPECIAL" DELIVERY
Design. Experience. "Making the world wobble on its axis a bit." One common denominator in all this: moving from "It works" to "It's special."

Thus Virginia Postrel, writing in her latest book, *The Substance of Style: How the Rise of Aesthetic Value Is Remaking Commerce, Culture, and Consciousness:* "Having spent a century or more focused on other goals— solving manufacturing problems, lowering costs, making goods and services widely available, increasing convenience, saving energy—we are increasingly engaged in making our world special. More people in more aspects of life are drawing pleasure and meaning from the way their persons, places, and things look and feel. *Whenever we have the chance, we're adding sensory, emotional appeal to ordinary function.*"

What's in a Word

Consider …

1. From *The Random House Dictionary of the English Language:*

experience (ik sp r' ens), n.v., -enced, -encing.

—n. 1. a particular instance of personally encountering or undergoing something: *My encounter with the bear in the woods was a frightening experience.* 2. the process or fact of personally observing, encountering, or undergoing something: *business experience.* 3. the observing, encountering, or undergoing of things generally as they occur in the course of time: *to learn from experience; the range of human experience.* 4. knowledge or practical wisdom gained from what one has observed, encountered, or undergone: *a man of experience.* 5. *Philos.* the totality of the cognitions given by perception; all that is perceived, understood, and remembered. —v.t. 6. to have experience of; meet with; undergo; feel: *to experience nausea.* 7. to learn by experience. 8. *experience religion,* to undergo a spiritual conversion by which one gains or regains faith in God. [1350-1400; ME < L *experientia*, equiv. to *experient-* (s. of *experi ns*, ptp. of *expir r* to try, test; see EX-, PERIL) + -*ia* n. suffix; see -ENCE] —ex pe'ri ence a ble, adj. --*ex pe'ri ence less*, adj.

—Syn. 6. encounter, know, endure, suffer. EXPERIENCE, UNDERGO refer to encountering situations, conditions, etc., in life, or to having certain sensations or feelings. EXPERIENCE implies being affected by what one meets with: *to experience a change of heart, bitter disappointment.* UNDERGO usually refers to the bearing or enduring of something hard, difficult, disagreeable, or dangerous: *to undergo severe hardships, an operation.*

2. *The Synonym Finder*, by J.I. Rodale:

experience, n. 1. affair, episode, ordeal, event, incident, occurrence, happening; encounter, transaction, adventure, *Sl.* trip; circumstance, case. 2. involvement, encountering, meeting, facing; exposure, observing, observation, perceiving, perception, impression; trials, vicissitudes, ups and downs. 3. life, existence, background, lifework; *U.S. Inf.* school of hard knocks. 4. wisdom, common sense; sophistication, enlightenment, knowledge, learning, cognizance, ken; know-how, savoir-faire.

—v. 5. encounter, meet, face; observe, perceive, apprehend; taste, sample, test, try; sense, feel; undergo, go through, get [s.t.] under one's belt; live through, endure, suffer through. 6. understand, learn about, become knowledgeable about, become familiar with, find out about; realize, discover, become enlightened, appreciate; know, cognize, *Chiefly Scot.* ken; assimilate, absorb, take in.

experienced, adj. 1. accomplished, practiced, skillful, polished, proficient, adept, good [at], *Fr. au fait*; knowledgeable, versed, prepared, qualified, well-grounded, trained, primed, ready; competent, fit, fitted, capable, able, efficient, *Sl.* on the ball; veteran, professional, *Inf.* knowing the ropes, *Sl.* savvy; expert, master, masterful, masterly. 2. mature, ripened, seasoned, salted; weathered, hardened, toughened, battle-scarred, Inf. through the mill, *Inf.* through the wringer; sophisticated, knowing, *Sl.* in the know, worldly, wordly-wise, *Sl.* wise, Inf. been around, initiated. 3. undergone, lived through, gone through, endured, suffered through; contacted, met, faced, observed, perceived; tasted, sampled, tested, tried; sensed, felt.

Keep considering ... these words and phrases from the above entries:

EPISODE
HAPPENING
ENCOUNTER
ADVENTURE
PERCEPTION
LIFE
EXISTENCE
TASTE
SENSE
LIVE THROUGH
UNDERGO
AFFECTED BY WHAT ONE MEETS WITH
SPIRITUAL CONVERSION

design

memorable experiences

How often do we use such words and phrases in business ... in our daily work life?

My answer: *seldom, rarely, never*. And yet, as the Value-Added Proposition of Business becomes more and more ... intangible ... such words become more and more ... relevant and practical and valuable.

Rebel Yell

A lot of people work for Harley-Davidson. The good news ... none of them are so silly as to believe that they "make *motorcycles.*"

If not "motorcycles," then what?

How about "experiences"?

A Harley Big Cheese put it this way: "What we sell is the ability for a 43-year-old accountant to dress in black leather, ride through small towns, and have people be afraid of him."

Harley-Davidson does not sell motorcyles

Club Med does not sell vacations

Say again?

It's the *experience*, stupid!

In particular, the experience that Harley calls the "Rebel Lifestyle."

Several years ago I ran into former Harley CEO Rich Teerlink, as we raced in opposite directions through the Atlanta airport. In the course of a couple of minutes of chatter, I asked him where he was coming from or going to. He replied he was just returning from a several-day training activity at ... Disney University. That's the place where Disney teaches us civilians how to ... Sprinkle Pixie Dust on our Clientèle. And Sprinkling Pixie Dust is precisely what Harley does to its Bikes and Bikers ... and what makes the firm ... So Damn Special.

(And don't you find it intriguing that the CEO of a Big *Mfg.* Co. was enrolled as "ordinary student" in a "mere" training program run by an *entertainment* company?)

So call it a semantic quibble. (If you must.) An "experience" instead of a "product." Yes, call it a semantic quibble. (If you dare.) But Teerlink's eventual success in changing Harley's "persona"—from "motorcycles" to "Rebel Lifestyle"—added Billions of Dollars to his company's stock-market capitalization.

Some quibble!

HEY, THAT'S A LIFESTYLE YOU'RE RIDING

Speaking of semantic quibbles: Rich Teerlink spent years sparring verbally with Wall Street wizards over the very definition of his company. "I pushed them over and over again," he told me, "to understand that we were a 'lifestyle company,' not a 'vehicle manufacturer.' "

Teerlink ultimately prevailed.

"Something More"

More and more companies are following in Harley's tracks.

"Club Med is more than just a resort," writes marketing maestro Jean-Marie Dru in his book *Disruption*. "It's a means of rediscovering oneself, or inventing an entirely new 'me.' "

Semantic frou-frou redux? Well, again, to the extent that Club Med succeeds in implanting this image (and

design

memorable experiences

arguably they've been quite successful), they are able to attract an entirely different clientèle to whom they can charge an entirely different price point—leading to an exceptional record of growth and profitability.

"We have identified a 'third place,' " Starbucks district manager Nancy Orsolini said in a TV interview. "And I really believe that sets us apart. The third place is that place that's not work or home. It's the place our customers come for refuge."

I don't know how the hell Starbucks does it! (Read founder Howard Schultz's book, *Pour Your Heart into It: How Starbucks Built a Company One Cup at a Time*, to find out a few of its secrets.) But the point is ... Starbucks *does* do it.

And it has transformed drinking an "innocent cup of java" into living the "Starbucks way of life." A way of life that, wittingly or not, many of us subscribe to ... whether that means taking a five-minute coffee break in an airport or spending an hour and a half reading the newspaper or editing a book chapter at a Starbucks in whatever town I happen to find myself in.

"Guinness as a brand is all about community," comments Ralph Ardill. "It's about bringing people together and sharing stories."

Ardill is a top boss at Imagination, a pioneering British design, marketing-services, and (yes) experiences-creating company. His firm completed an eye-popping assignment

---

SOMETHING BASIC: CLEAN UP YOUR ACT!

A great experience offering is about "something more." Yes. To be sure. But it is also about ... something basic. As basic as keeping your establishment tidy.

September 2004. I was at a giant shopping mall one weekend, and strolled into an outlet of a Renowned Retailer.

Experience marketing? This retailer "gets" it. And does it ... very well.

But on this Saturday ... *this place looked like a disaster area.*

It was a very busy day. The place was packed with customers. (Congratulations, Renowned Retailer.) But it had gotten very messy in the course of the day. Goods scattered. Goods

in untidy stacks. Trash on the floor. Boxes stacked unattractively near the checkout desk. To me the space *screamed* ... "We Don't Give a Shit."

A Great Experience has many attributes. But right near the head of the line is: "WE CARE!" And a key part of saying "We care" is to ... KEEP IT CLEAN!

There is no excuse whatsoever for sloppiness.

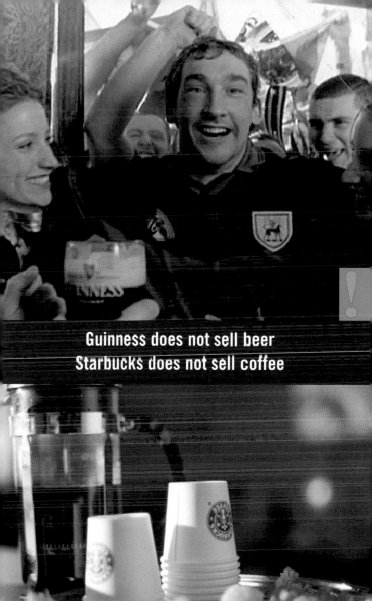

Guinness does not sell beer
Starbucks does not sell coffee

for Guinness—the Guinness Storehouse. Situated at company HQ in Dublin, it amounts to a sort of home port for ... the Soul of Guinness.

Think about it. Harley-Davidson does *not* sell motorcycles. Starbucks does *not* sell coffee. Club Med does *not* sell vacations. And Guinness does *not* sell beer.

Have you ever *ridden* on a Harley, *been* to Club Med, *stopped* at a Starbucks, *imbibed* a Guinness? There *is* "something more" there. Moreover, I believe that this "something more" is ... the Essence of the Enterprise ... the Fundamental Basis for its Value Added.

GET A "LIFE"

Okay, okay. You're skeptical. ("Those Guinness bastards sell beer by the pint, for heaven's sake!") That skepticism is totally *appropriate.*

Because most companies trying to pull off this "experience thing" will fail miserably. They won't get it. They'll add a touch here. A touch there.

But in the case of Harley and Club Med and Starbucks and Guinness, the "experience"—the "way of life"—is the damn enterprise.

This "experience" thing is ... extremist. Not a dab of "delight" here. Nor a pinch of "amusement" there. But ... An Entirely Different Way of Life.

What "Experience" Does for "Brown"

Winston Churchill had a thing about the color brown. "I cannot pretend to be impartial about colors. I rejoice with the brilliant ones and am genuinely sorry for the poor brown." I agree completely and wholeheartedly ... most of the time.

Then something comes along that makes me see brown ... differently. A new company logo. A new series of advertisements. A new branding campaign that began a few years ago. One that I simply *love*.

WAKE UP AND SMELL THE ... *EXPERIENCE*

Another blast from *The Substance of Style,* by Virginia Postrel: "With its carefully conceived mix of colors and textures, aromas and music, Starbucks is more indicative of our era than the iMac. It is to the age of aesthetics what McDonald's was to the age of convenience or Ford was to the age of mass production—the touchstone success story, the exemplar of all that is good and bad about the aesthetic imperative. ... 'Every Starbucks store is carefully designed to enhance the quality of everything the customers see, touch, hear, smell or taste,' writes CEO Howard Schultz."

Namely: "WHAT CAN BROWN DO FOR YOU?"

Brown, of course, is UPS. And I love its new "look" ... its new "everything" ... on so many dimensions. Brown is the most dreary of colors. Almost the anti-color color. And yet those "plain brown trucks" have come to mean an awful lot in our lives.

But now UPS is working overtime to get way—as in *way, way, way*—beyond the "brown trucks driven by guys in brown shorts" image. UPS is "repositioning" itself. (BIG TIME.) It aims to become a Full Scale Partner in Logistics and Supply Chain Excellence—a partner that can serve as a lynchpin in many a corporate strategy.

There is a ... *phenomenon* ... UPS wants to sell you. And what a lovely way to describe it: BROWN. It is a phenomenon that has to do with Taking Full Care of a Huge Part of Your Business Life in a Way that Will Allow You to Add Incredible Value for Your Beloved Customer.

I cotton to the UPS story for another reason relative to this analysis. The previous examples come from the world of consumer goods— Harley, Club Med, Starbucks, Guinness. But UPS is in the business of selling ... *professional services*. "WHAT CAN BROWN DO FOR YOU?" is aimed directly at the business customer.

Plot Power

Freeman Thomas co-designed the new VW Beetle, and designed the Audi TT. Now he does his thing for Chrysler. Thomas talks about the exciting Plymouth Prowler: "Car

Plot Power!

design

memorable experiences

COLOR ME PROFITABLE
Colors are funny things. Powerful, too.

Coca-Cola "owns" RED. And Kodak "owns" (or, alas, "owned") YELLOW.

Likewise, especially with its "What Can Brown Do for You?" campaign,

UPS aims to cement its ownership of ... BROWN.

The same kind of "color theory" is being applied at Home Depot, where boss Bob Nardelli aims to make "The ORANGE Box" synonymous with solutions to all home-care problems.

And then there's BP, which is trying to alter the entire perception of an industry (and itself) by "owning" ... GREEN.

Hmmm.

Color may just be the ultimate ... experience.

designers need to create a story. Every car provides an opportunity to create an adventure. ... The Prowler makes you smile. Why? Because it's focused. It has a plot, a reason for being, a passion."

I'm not much of a car guy, and I'm not particularly interested in the ins and outs of that Prowler. I am interested in ... once again ... words.

Consider these words from Mr. Thomas:

design

STORY.
ADVENTURE.
SMILE.
FOCUS.
PLOT.
REASON FOR BEING.
PASSION.
I LOVE *ALL* THOSE WORDS.

memorable experiences

Score Tactics: The Plot, Thickened

Soon after reading that quote by Freeman Thomas, I had an opportunity to test the power of this idea. I was working with a mid-size retail enterprise that aimed to dramatically improve its catalog business. The products offered were fine and dandy. The company has an excellent and widely respected history. But it seemed as though "tactical marketing initiative" after "tactical marketing initiative" was falling flat.

In a seminar with the company's executive group, I suggested that they look at their catalog ... and think about the "experience"/"plot" that it conjured up. I stuck my neck out and provided a personal assessment of a bunch of catalogs that I'd randomly grabbed on the way to the seminar. In fact, I audaciously graded them on a scale of 1 to 10 on "plot." Scoring key: 1 = "dreary and pointless"; 10 = "a plot that sizzles!"

WILLIAMS-SONOMA. 5. Used to be a clear 10. Williams-Sonoma reinvented the American kitchen—along with Julia Child. The products Williams-Sonoma provides today are excellent. But for me the "plot" has lost its edge. "La différence" is missing. In other words: What's the Point? What's the Plot?

CRATE AND BARREL. 8. Crate and Barrel, at least until its recent Marimekko incarnation, wasn't very colorful, which leaves me cold. On the other hand, Crate and Barrel clearly has a ... Distinct Point of View. A plot. And it does a damn good job with that "plot."

SMITH & HAWKEN. 8+. The product, again, is fine and dandy. The story is great. Smith & Hawken sells a certain "lifestyle." And sells it well, on the whole.

SHARPER IMAGE. 9. Sometimes I like what I see. Sometimes I hate what I see. But I know what the hell the story is going to be—and I can't wait to see the next episode. (That is, the next catalog.)

L.L.BEAN. 3. L.L.Bean probably deserves a higher score. My negativism is partially a nostalgia trip gone sour. I well remember L.L.Bean when it had one hell of a "plot"! I remember those days, years and years ago, when I simply couldn't wait to get my hands on my Dad's L.L.Bean catalog—even if I was in no position financially to order a damn thing. It was a wild, scintillating, Starbucks-level story and approach to life. The products are still damn good. (I have a few, so I know.) But the story has lost its edge.

design

memorable experiences

"... mobile sculpture, which, coincidentall

When my clients and I got beyond dry analytics, and started talking "story," "plot," "experience" ... the nature of our discussion changed dramatically from what it had been before. Discussing "brand power" and "strategic coherence" did little or nothing for them. Talking "plot" at Williams-Sonoma led to almost a shouting match in which points of view were offered at machine-gun pace.

> **THE EXPERIENCE OF ... LANGUAGE**
>
> *For participants in that seminar, thinking in terms of "plot" was an invaluable exercise—or should I say "an invaluable experience"? Because language is an experience, too. Words per se ... words like "story," "plot," and yes, "experience" ... make all the difference. They change the way we respond to a product, a service—or a catalog marketing seminar.*

Car Art

Bob Lutz is single-handedly, it seems, changing the look, feel, taste, touch, smell, and (yes) plot of things at General Motors, a formerly sluggish industrial giant. And he's doing so along the dimension of ... experience.

"I see us as being in the art business," Lutz said once. "Art, entertainment and mobile sculpture, which, coincidentally, also happens to provide transportation."

Where Lutz operates is where the rubber meets the road ... literally and figuratively.

lso happens to provide transportation"

You can write off the Lutz statement as so much smoke and mirrors. Or you can say, as I believe, that it gets to the heart of change at GM. A shift toward focusing on the automotive *experience*. (Not just on low finance charges.) An understanding that one is in the "art, entertainment, and mobile sculpture business"— which also provides basic transportation.

Other car companies are getting "it"—following two decades of "quality-is-all." We're starting to remember that our car is ... who we are, a keystone of our identity.

And the impact ripples outward through the industry. Consider Harman International, maker of ultra high-end sound systems. The automobile industry in general, and Lexus in particular, is central to its exceptionally effective strategy. Company founder Sidney Harman has gone so far as to say, "Lexus sells its cars as containers for our sound system. It's marvelous."

AND WHILE WE'RE AT IT, HERE'S AN ENGINE
Bob Lutz and Sidney Harmon are defining the front edge of ... the biggest auto-industry transformation in decades.

Consider this headline from a November 2002 *Newsweek* article: "Living Room, to Go: Cars of the future will be sanctuaries, with mood lighting, aroma therapy, and massage seats. For long drives: movies and popcorn."

Now, *that's* an experience!

Sounds a bit self-serving. (It is.)

Sounds a bit outrageous. (It is.)

But I'm not sure he's all wet. (He's not.)

Hundreds of billions of dollars are at stake in what is still an enormous industry, and the shift back to "cool cars" (terrific experiences!) is very noticeable.

Have Your Cake—And Experience It, Too

Our tour guides Joe Pine and Jim Gilmore summarize their argument in terms of a value-added "experience ladder." "Raw materials" are at the base. Next up, "goods." Then "services." Then ... scraping the value-added sky ... "experiences."

Let's examine this ever-so-potent notion in a somewhat humble fashion. My friend Tim Sanders is a senior executive at Yahoo! The irrepressible Mr. Sanders (an experience himself) is responsible for the "experience" part of the business. (Which is most of what Yahoo! is about.) Tim loves to describe "all this" in terms of the humble birthday cake.

Think of Cakes Through Four Generations:

1940: The raw-materials economy ...

Grandma spends a buck or so to buy flour, sugar, and other "raw materials." (Okay, flour and sugar are both industrial processed goods—but you know what I mean.) Using those raw materials, Grandma produces a birthday cake. *($1.)*

1955: The goods economy ...

Ma goes down to the local Albertsons, spends a couple of bucks, and makes the cake from a packaged industrial good ... Betty Crocker cake mix. *($2.)*

1970: The service economy ...

Bakeries are available to ordinary folks, not just the rich and super-rich. So Mom heads to the bakery at birthday time and shells out $10 for a professionally baked cake. *($10.)*

1990: The experience economy ...

Dad is in charge of the kid's birthday now. And the kid lays down the law: "I'm having a party, Dad. It's going

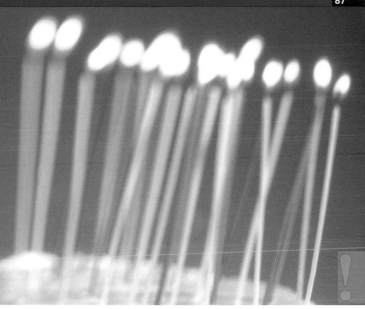

to be at Chuck E. Cheese, and I'm bringing my pals."
Dad obliges, and forks over a C-note ... for the Chuck E.
Cheese "experience." *($100.)*

A silly example, perhaps. But is it so different from
Starbucks? The most interesting part of this example—
and it can be replayed chapter and verse for Starbucks
or Harley-Davidson or UPS—is that the Big Leap takes
place when the "experience dimension" is added to the
mix. Remember in the case of the cake: $1.00 to $2.00,
$2.00 to $10.00, $10.00 to $100.00. The Chuck E.
Cheese "experience bit" added the last $90!

MEASURING UP

*Like many others, I believe that "what gets measured gets done." Thus,
we need new metrics for a new era.*

    The Raw Materials Economy: *Raw Quantity—a Practical Measure!*
    The Goods Economy: *Six Sigma—an Excellent Measure!*
    The Services Economy: *Customer Satisfaction—a Brilliant Measure!*
    The Experiences Economy: *Customer Success—the Ultimate Measure!*

    *"Customer success" in "transforming your image" ... following a
visit to Club Med. "Customer success" in "re-inventing your lifestyle"
... following purchase of a Harley. "Customer success" in "logistics
transformation" ... following a little help from the folks at UPS.*

No Limits I: It's Geek to Me

Joe Pine tells a wonderful story about a next-door neighbor of his in Minneapolis. Robert Stephens owns a small business that installs computer-telecommunications systems. So-called "local area networks," or LANs. The original company name was to the point: LAN Installation Company.

Fine.

Accurate.

To the point.

But over the back fence, Joe and his techie neighbor got to talking about the "experience thing." (Quite a push for a "techie.") To make a long story short, LAN Installation Company morphed ... hold onto your hat ... into *The Geek Squad*. That is, the talented techies, who had always done good technical work, now emphasized the fun, energy, excellence, reliability ... *the experience provided* ... behind what they do. Now they cruise to client sites in circa-1974 ice-cream trucks, painted black, and wear black suits with white socks and pants legs that are three inches too short.

And (to continue making this long story relatively short) the company quickly grew from having 2 percent of Minnesota's LAN installation business to having 30 percent of it. (Wow!)

Lots of things happened in the process, beyond the scope of this chapter—which is just meant to introduce the "experience" notion. For example, employees are far more turned on by being a member of a "Geek Squad" than of a "LAN Installation Company." It's not that they

design

memorable experiences

BUILD AN *EXPERIENCE*
In 1997, after a grand 25-year career at May Department Stores, Maxine Clark opened her first Build-A-Bear Workshop location in St Louis, Missouri. By 2004, she was heading a $300 million company that's growing

like Topsy, both in the United States and abroad.

When I visited the company Web site (www. buildabear.com) in the fall of 2004, what I saw made me go out on a limb and call it ... THE BEST WEB SITE I'VE VISITED! It passes all the tests: Easy

to use! Informative as hell! Incredibly interactive! Cool! Fun!

In short: It's an ENGAGING EXPERIENCE... not merely a "service."

weren't technically competent before. They were and still are. But now they have the self-image of being … *flying, roving, awesomely competent problem solvers relative to a set of technology issues.*

No Limits II: (Don't) Leave It to Beaver

I was thinking about "all this" when I happened upon a *Wall Street Journal* article in mid-2002. It turns out that New England has seen an extraordinary share of its previously open grazing land returned to forests. One implication: an explosion of wildlife, which sometimes mixes very uncomfortably with nearby human neighbors.

Beavers, in particular, have become a problem. If you've ever had a farm pond (I have three), you know that in short order a beaver can destroy any damn tree-like thing it needs, and then plug up the pond, causing the worst sort of flooding.

People who "deal with beavers" have historically been called "trappers." And there are, indeed, trappers alive and well in New England. In recent times, trappers have netted $20 per beaver pelt. Transforming "beavers" into "pelts" is the trapper's historic … "value proposition." (An instance of the "raw materials" economy?)

But along comes a "problem." Too many relatively well-off people living near too much wildlife. So the wise trapper decides he's no longer a "trapper". Now he becomes a … yup! … *Wildlife Damage-Control Professional.* And … a W.D.C.P. (Wildlife Damage-Control Professional) can charge $150 … not a mere $20 … for the "removal of a problem beaver."

design

memorable experiences

A REALLY (BIG!) SHOW
In Las Vegas in 2003, I had a free night. I pulled some strings, and went to my first performance of Cirque du Soleil.
WOW!
I'll never be the same!
Now I *own* the Gold Standard for Experiences.

But more than that, I've had a practical business *epiphany.* (I try to avoid that word. But sometimes it's justified.) I just don't see why (say) a business process re-design project shouldn't be held to the Cirque du Soleil Standard.
You are, like me, a

proud professional, right? Why should your or my standard for a project (that is, a *performance* … an **experience**) be less than that of the leaders and cast members of Cirque du Soleil?

"Wildlife Damage-Control Professional?"

Some nouveau residents, however, love their beavers, and wish to keep them around. But they don't want that noxious flooding. Our wily W.D.C.P. charges a full $750 to $1,000 for providing flood control piping ... so that the beavers can stay ... and so that the floods will go away.

Welcome to the "experience economy"

Love that.

Welcome to the "experience economy."

Instead of a Redneck-Totin'-a-Gun who makes 20 bucks a pelt ... we now have a Wildlife Damage-Control Professional Services and Solutions Provider who bills out at $1,000 to deliver an "experience."

(Ah, life.)

Let's Get Metaphysical!

Getting started in the "experience business" is (mostly) about frame of mind. The requisite transformation is not easy. "Most managers," writes Danish marketing expert Jesper Kunde, in his book *Unique Now ... or Never*, "have no idea how to add value [to a market] in the metaphysical world. But that is what the market will cry out for in the future. There is no lack of [physical] products to choose between."

design

memorable experiences

SHE'S THE BOSS (OR SHOULD BE)

Just an idea ...

Old Economy = raw materials, along with basic goods and services. Dominated by men. By male thinking and male ideas.

New Economy = value-added experiences. Dominated by women. By female thinking and female ideas.

As Faith Popcorn and Lys Marigold note in their brilliant book *EVEolution*, "Women don't buy brands. They join them."

In other words, the "experience" idea is one that women take to naturally. Men ... not necessarily so.

More women in leadership positions makes sense. One reason: The nature of the "products delivered" by more and more companies ... that is, "experiences" and "solutions" ... plays to strengths that women inherently bring to the table. We are, quite possibly, entering into a ... Women's Economy.

For more on "the Women's Economy," see the companion volumes *Essentials: Leadership* and *Essentials: Trends*.

Kunde's exemplars include Nokia, Nike, Lego, and Virgin ... all Masters of Experience ... all makers and marketers of physical products that have a metaphysical presence. But how many leaders are taking those examples (and examples of the sort that I provided above) seriously ... "seriously" to the point of fundamentally altering enterprise strategy? How many of the Big Guys (and it's no coincidence that most of them are guys and not gals) are comfortable dealing with Kunde's "metaphysical world"?

"M3" PLAYER?

Kunde pushes his (already "out there") idea a step further. Tomorrow's CEOs, he insists, will have to trade their MBA degrees for M3 degrees: from Master of Business Administration to ... Master of Metaphysical Management. I do not disagree with him. Not at all.

Feet, Don't Fail Me Now

A couple of years ago, I attended a Big Retailer's day-long strategy session. I heard a lot of talk along the lines of "Thrash the competition" and "Go for the gold." I was impressed by a striking array of merchandising initiatives that participants said would "bring in the quarter." My head reeled from all the new programs being launched.

But throughout the day, my foot kept wiggling. Something—what?—felt oddly off. My day done, I moved on to another city, and then home. But, at least metaphorically, I couldn't still the wiggling in my foot.

ESPRIT DE "CORE"

What makes an experience an *experience* is that it has ... at its center ... some sense of unified whole. Some sense of ... *design*.

From *Businessworld* of India: "HAVE MBAs KILLED OFF MARKETING? Prof Rajeev Batra says: 'What these times call for is more creative and breakthrough reengineering of product and service benefits, but we don't train people to act like that.' The way marketing is taught across business schools is far too analytical and data-driven. 'We've taken away the emphasis on creativity and big ideas that characterize real marketing breakthroughs.' In India there is an added problem: most senior marketing jobs have been traditionally dominated by MBAs. Santosh Desai, vice president, McCann Erickson, an MBA himself, believes in India engineer-MBAs, armed with this Lego-like approach, tend to reduce marketing into neat components. 'This reductionist thinking runs counter to the idea that great brands must have a core, unifying idea.' "

design

memorable experiences

THIS IS A
BIG
DEAL

I'd be exaggerating if I said "the answer" came to me in a flash, but it more or less did. Our retail pals had sliced and diced and talked about everything but ... the thing that matters. *The whole shebang, the adventure, the story, the plot, the "holistic" experience.*

What the hell is it like, from parking lot to checkout counter, for customers to "imbibe" a given store in this retailer's chain? Where's the pixie dust?

The CEO of this company, trust me, is not a metaphysical sort of guy. But I wrote him an impassioned letter. I might well have called it "The Tale of the Wiggling Foot That Would Not Be Stilled."

Who knows, but I think I was on to something. Something big. Even enormous.

Are You Experienced?

Re-read this chapter. Look at the examples. Think of other examples. Play with this word ... *experience.*

Then what?

Should you hire a theater director to join your accounting department? Or your product-development department? Or your marketing department?

Perhaps.

Think experience. *Talk* experience. *Consider* examples of experience. *Analyze* those examples. And remember:

1. This is not a semantic quibble. It is ... the Essence of Life in the New Economy.

2. Billions upon billions of dollars are at stake for big companies. And, relatively speaking, the same high stakes apply to the individual accountant ... and to the beaver trapper turned Wildlife Damage-Control Professional.

3. THIS IS A BIG DEAL.

NEW LENS ON LIFE
Experiences. I have seldom if ever been so affected by a single word.

I now view positively everything through a new lens. "What's the experience like?" is so ... very ... different from "Were you satisfied with 'the service'?"

I lament my inability to transmit my enthusiasm for this idea to you to the fullest, deepest extent. I dearly want you to become as inflamed by this idea as I have become inflamed. I want you never to view any transaction through any lens other than ... Experience Magnification.

TOP 10 TO-DOs

1. *Experience ... language.* Recalibrate your vocabulary. Pore over the definition of that word: "experience." Let its many permutations ... wash over you.

2. *Experience ... the world.* Cull your memory banks for moments when everything (time, place, mood, people) seemed to click. Take notes, learn, adapt, adopt.

3. *Experience ... "life."* Get over the notion that, say, "Starbucks sells coffee." It doesn't. Not really. It sells an entire Way of Life. So: What "Life" do you sell?

4. *Experience ... the intangible.* Grasp the ungraspable. (The difference between a Harley and some other motorcycle is not something ... you can put a finger on.)

5. *Experience ... "more."* Say that you're in the auto-parts retailing business. Sit down and describe everything that you do for customers. Do not use the words "auto," "part," or "retail."

6. *Experience ... plot.* Tell the *story* that your company evokes through everything that it does. Next: Grade the plot of that story. Do you "pass"? With "honors"?

7. *Experience ... value.* Apply the "birthday cake" exercise to your business, and calculate the benefits of climbing ... the Value-Added Experience Ladder.

8. *Experience ... your job.* Dig out your official "job description," dust it off, and rewrite it from the ground up with an eye to ... what *experience* you provide—or could provide.

9. *Experience ... your company.* Consider your company's "value offering" from the vantage point of ... the Entire Customer Experience. Break it down, interaction by interaction. Then: Reinvent it!

10. *Experience ... design.* Find a product whose design you completely adore—an iPod, say. Now mull over the many ways that your experience of that product goes far (far!) beyond how cool it looks. Mantra: A great Design = A great Experience.

!

COOL FRIEND: Tom Kelley

Tom Kelley is general manager of IDEO, a leading design consultancy that specializes in product development and innovation. Along with his brother, IDEO founder David Kelley, he has been responsible for the firm's business development, marketing, human resources, and operations. Below are some remarks that he made in connection with the publication of his book, **The Art of Innovation: Lessons in Creativity from IDEO, America's Leading Design Firm** *(2001).*

We'll go into a meeting in which there's, let's say, six people who have each spent 20 years working in [an] industry. And then we have to help them innovate. Well, that's really hard. They've got 120 years collective experience and I'm brand-new to their industry. But one of our biggest secrets is our ability to take our human-factors specialists that tend to have degrees in areas like cognitive psychology, and go to their customers, sometimes even to their non-customers, in real-life settings, and watch them using the products. You see what works; you see what doesn't work.

And if those companies have not done this kind of observation before, we can almost always see something they haven't noticed, of if they have noticed they haven't valued. They've just assumed it away. And there we'll get our final epiphanies. That's where the magic in the process comes from.

* *

[N]o one seems to modify or design a car for use as a rental car. Why is that? What's the total fleet of rental cars in America? It's gigantic.

In your own car, for instance, you have a muscle memory of where things are. You know where to reach to turn on the windshield wiper, you know where the door handle is, and things like that. But in a rental car you don't. ... You're in the rental car, you've just turned off the engine, you've just turned out the lights, you're now in a dark parking lot. It can take me up to 20 minutes to find that door handle. Because it used to be ... this big hunk of metal sticking out of the door and you bumped into it every time you moved your leg. Whereas now—and I think it's safer this way—it's recessed into the door. But where, you know? Is it high, is it low, is it forward? You're reduced to fumbling around. And for about a nickel, they could put a little LED in there that would stay on for, say, 30 seconds—no impact on battery life—that would light up right behind where the door handle is and you'd find it every time.

* *

My favorite thing we worked on is the Heartstream Defibrillator. It is this device that's now on most airplanes, that basically saves your life if you go into cardiac arrest. It's got those two paddles. ... [B]asically, if you go into cardiac arrest, you have six minutes to live. Your chances of survival go down 10 percent every minute. And you're not at 100 percent at the beginning either, because you're lying on the floor, not breathing. And so, even if you've got a heart surgeon in the seat next to you on the plane, they cannot save you unless they have a defibrillator.

And so we helped with this device. We worked on the interface. It's this hilariously simple one-two-three interface that you'd have to ideally call the "Wet Nap interface"—an interface so simple that the instructions say "Open and use." And partly because the product is so simple, a lot of people who did not have medical training have been able to save lives. I think up to 60 lives have been saved with this device so far. So we took something that's very complex, and made it so simple that my daughter, when she was six years old, could make it work. ...

There's people that would be dead today that are alive because this device was there.

* *

We have this expression: "Focus on the verbs, not the nouns." Meaning that, especially early in a project, if you focus too much on the thing, it will lead you astray. ... [T]his thing of thinking verbs, not nouns is definitely an idea about designing an experience as opposed to designing a thing. And when we're doing our human-factors observations, we're not watching the thing; we're watching humans and what kind of experience, good or bad, they have interacting with it.

* *

[R]ecently we've had the chance to actually design experiences outright, where there is no physical thing. With Amtrak, for example, we worked with designing the service strategy for their Acela Express Service in the Northeast Corridor.

And at the Steelcase office building at Four Columbus Circle, in New York, we helped design the experience of buying furniture at that location. And there's very little physical embodiment to it. We went through the process and watched what people do as they figure out what office furniture to get, and we looked for ways to improve And they tell us that people are staying longer in the space than they used to, and they're buying more. So that's the kind of thing that makes the client happy. ...

I think one of the best first-time-visit experiences I've ever had was at this building. I don't believe IDEO designed this portion of the experience, but you step out of the elevator, and this very pleasant woman gets up from behind her desk and says, "Welcome to Steelcase. Please have a seat over in the cafe and help yourself to coffee." And then you go over there, and it's this beautiful cafe. It could be a commercial restaurant. It's got a panoramic view over Central Park. And I'm thinking, gee, this is pretty nice. I feel completely welcomed by first, the staff, but second, the space. Even if I have to wait 15 minutes there, hey, I'm a pretty happy guy. And so, that's a particularly well-designed experience for a first-time visitor.

* *

Kids are more creative than adults, for the most part, because they're not inhibited.

What happens in a lot of organizations, especially large organizations, is that people get inhibited. They start getting rules: "You can't make fun of the boss. You can't tell a joke that might offend him or her. Can't put up your own artwork in the cubicle. Can't do this."

And so if you can turn back the clock a little bit, to your youth, that will help recreate some of that lost creativity. ... In kindergarten, everybody knows it is perfectly okay to shove all the desks to the outer side of the room so that you can have some big play area in the center, then to scoot them all back together when you want to do some art work together. Then spin them a little to the side when you want to work individually. Nobody feels like you have to ask permission to do that. That's just kids doing what comes naturally.

And so if companies would have less built-in furniture in their offices, it would free them up to do more things.

* *

Think about business calendars. Businesspeople throughout history had calendars that they kept track of their appointments on. Right? But for a long time, it was this thing that sat on their desks. And their secretaries ... would come in and write something on it, and when someone wanted to check someone's schedule, they went to that desk and looked at the calendar.

Then Day-Timers and the like came along and turned that into something much more personal. Partly they made it portable, but it became this indispensable tool. And now, Palm and others have made it electronic. It's actually, to me, more useful than the Day-Timer, because you can do different sorts of searches and it's got next year's calendar, last year's, and all that. And this becomes a very personal thing. ...

If people can develop a product or a service that is so personal that it feels like your thing, I think that is certainly one avenue to developing brand loyalty or strengthening your relationship with the customer.

4

EXPERIENCES-PLUS: EMBRACING THE "DREAM BUSINESS"

!

Contrasts

Was	Is
"Mere" experiences *(good enough for Chapter 3)*	Wild Imaginings ... and Dreams Fulfilled
Things done well	Things not thought possible
"It's damn good"	"You can do *that?*"
Pleased	Elated
Surprised	Stunned
"Selling to customers"	Tempting customers
"I'm not sure I need it."	"I GOTTA HAVE IT. *NOW.*"

!Rant

We are not prepared ...

We are still mired in Old Economy, OLD PRODUCT THINKING. • But we *must*—all of us!—come to grips, "strategically," with the fact that **WINNERS IN THE NEW ECONOMY WILL BE ... MASTERS OF THE DREAM BUSINESS.**

!Vision

I imagine ...

"IMPOSSIBLE" DREAMS THAT BECOME (MORE THAN) POSSIBLE.

Enterprises with the ... *COURAGE* ... to reject the "zero defects" nostrum.

Value propositions that **go way, way beyond "products" and "services"** (two drab terms that we will no longer need to use).

He's Just Dreamy

I love the "experience" idea. (I tried to convey some
dimensions of my flagrant love affair in the last chapter.)
For many people, that idea is a big stretch ... especially
compared with the normal "business" way of looking at
products and services. And yet perhaps we can stretch
our minds even further. Much further?

The stakes are high ... billions upon billions of
dollars. (Again.)

So ... next vocabulary s-t-r-e-t-c-h: *dreams*.

Now, that word goes far outside this old civil
engineer's comfort zone—and this old civil engineer was
already reeling from our visit to the ethereal-but-still-
hard-dollar realm of "experiences."

The power of the "dream" idea was revealed to me
when I was fortunate enough to sit in on a presentation
in Mexico City by former Ferrari North America CEO Gian
Luigi Longinotti-Buitoni. Dreams are his shtick.

Dream products.
Dream fulfillment.
Dream marketing.
Dream provision.

Consider ... very carefully ... the following statement
by Mr. Longinotti-Buitoni: "A dream is a complete
moment in the life of a client. Important experiences that
tempt the client to commit substantial resources. The
essence of the desires of the consumer. The opportunity
to help clients become what they want to be."

What marvelous words! "Complete moment."
"Tempt." "Commit." "Essence." "Desires." And,
summing it all up: "the opportunity to help clients
become what they want to be."

"DREAM" LANGUAGE
From Rodale's *The
Synonym Finder*:
"*dream, n.* 1. vision,
nightmare; apparition,
will-o'-the-wisp, ignis
fatuus, chimera, fairy;
phantom, shade, specter,
ghost, wraith, incubus,
succubus, bugbear;
fantasy, phantasm,
phantasma, *Lit.* fantasia,
Inf. pipe dream, romance;
figment, figment of
the imagination, fiction,
invention, fabrication;
visualization,
envisagement,
hallucination, mirage,
illusion, delusion; shadow,
vapor, nothingness."

design | experiences-plus

I'm not sure I fully understand all of those words. But I think I sort of "get" them. And I suspect that if I did understand them fully ... I would ... gasp.

Yes, the right word: *gasp*.

Tragedy of the "Common"

Longinotti-Buitoni distinguishes between "common products" and "dream products." To wit:

COMMON PRODUCT		DREAM PRODUCT
Maxwell House	... *versus* ...	Starbucks
BVD	... *versus* ...	Victoria's Secret
Payless	... *versus* ...	Ferragamo
Hyundai	... *versus* ...	Ferrari
Suzuki	... *versus* ...	Harley-Davidson
Atlantic City	... *versus* ...	Acapulco
New Jersey	... *versus* ...	California
Carter	... *versus* ...	Kennedy
Connors	*versus*	Pelé
CNN	... *versus* ...	"Who Wants to Be a Millionaire"

design

experiences-plus

There is nothing necessarily wrong with the first part of each of those pairs. Each offers a solid, workaday response to some need or another. But the second part all of that "stuff" carries a dreamlike power that goes far, far beyond the realm of mere "need fulfillment."

Adventures in ... "Dreamketing"

Longinotti-Buitoni preaches "marketing of dreams"—an idea that he compresses into a word of his own coinage: *dreamketing*. It's rather klutzy, especially when applied

---

WISE TO THE WORD
Winston Churchill said, "We shape our buildings. Thereafter, they shape us." I say: "We shape our words. Thereafter, they shape us."

Something special happens when we talk about "dreams," or "dreamketing," or "experiences." We view the world through a new lens.

True, I speak and write for a living. Words are therefore *everything* to me. But one of my goals in this book—one of my principal goals—is to turn you into the same sort of Certified Word Fanatic that I am.

to such an aesthetically rich topic. Nonetheless, I find myself reeled in by it.

Dreamketing: Touching the client's dreams.
Dreamketing: The art of telling stories and entertaining.
Dreamketing: Promoting the dream, not the product.
Dreamketing: Building the brand around the Main Dream.
Dreamketing: Building "buzz," "hype," a "cult."

Longinotti-Buitoni also provides hard financial data that demonstrate ... clearly ... that what he calls "dream" products provide (along with fulfillment to customers) returns to shareholders that are miles beyond the returns from "common" products.

This is not pie in the sky. It's a hard-core business message, delivered by a practical businessman who has created or enhanced some extraordinary franchises. I think he's well worth listening to—especially in a world where Value Added derives increasingly from Great Design and Awesome Experiences and other features that go (far) beyond ... (mere) functionality.

design

experiences-plus

EXTREME DREAM

Meta-message of this book: Focusing on functionality is ... dysfunctional. Most everything "works." And damn well at that. So what goes beyond "works well"?

Excitement. *That's what.*
Surprise. *That's what.*
Things not thought possible. *That's what.*
My point (again): to urge you to "raise the bar." UP. WAY UP.
Think Design. Think Beautiful Systems.
Drop "products" and "services."
Substitute "experiences." Substitute "dreams."

Project: Dream

I hope to sign you up! I hope that you'll play with (right term) the ideas in this chapter—and consider applying them to your current project.

(In finance.)
(In purchasing.)
(In human resources.)
(In information systems.)

Here are your instructions: RE-IMAGINE THAT PROJECT. DO NOT REST ... UNTIL THAT PROJECT PASSES THE TESTS OF DREAMKETING SET FORTH BY GIAN LUIGI LONGINOTTI-BUITONI. UNTIL YOU'VE TURNED THAT "SUZUKI" TRAINING COURSE INTO A "HARLEY-DAVIDSON" TRAINING COURSE ... OR THAT "MAXWELL HOUSE" BUSINESS PROCESS INTO A "STARBUCKS" BUSINESS PROCESS.

Think about a staff department ... in your company. Shouldn't its "training course" Radically Change the Life View of *Every* Participant?

YES. (DAMN IT.)

Shouldn't the next "business process re-engineering project" be an ... Exercise in Dream Fulfillment?

YES. (DAMN IT.)

Why bother with a project unless it is a Dreamketing Project ... unless, that is, it will Dramatically Alter the Perspective of both Designer-Provider and User-Client?

Key words:

DRAMATICALLY.
ALTER.
PERSPECTIVE.

design

experiences-plus

SHARED DREAM

The "Dream" theme is ... taking flight.

Here's Rolf Jensen, head of the Copenhagen Institute for Future Studies, writing in his book *The Dream Society: How the Coming Shift from Information to Imagination Will Transform Your Business:* "The sun is setting on the Information Society—even before we

have fully adjusted to its demands as individuals and as companies. We have lived as hunters and as farmers, we have worked in factories, and now we live in an information-based society whose icon is the computer. We stand facing the fifth type of society: the Dream Society! ... The Dream Society is emerging this very instant—the

shape of the future is visible today. Right now is the time for decisions— before the major portion of consumer purchases are made for emotional, nonmaterialistic reasons. Future products will have to appeal to our hearts, not to our heads. ... Now is the time to add emotional value to products and services."

Dreams!
Dreams!
Dreams!

Nike *More than high performance gear. Try: The promise of a High Performance Life.*

Porsche *Tough to drive at times? Yes. But who cares: I AM MY PORSCHE.*

Armani *We wear Armani. We become Armani.*

Google *It's a ubiquitous search engine. As one commentator put it, "Google is a bit like God."*

Virgin *Use Virgin. Be cool.*

Intel Centrino *An invisible chip? No! The guarantee of a cutting-edge life enhanced by sexy technology.*

Dream Logic

How do you implement a Dream? For those who seek to turn their project team into ... a Dream Team ... Mr. Longinotti-Buitoni offers some specific advice:

- Maximize your value added by fulfilling the dreams of your clients.
- Invest only in what is valuable for your client.
- Don't let short-term results weaken the long-term value of your brand.
- Balance rigorous control of the financial endeavor with the emotional management of your brand.
- Build a financial structure that allows risk-taking: NO RISKS—NO DREAMS.
- Establish long-term "price power" in order to avoid the trap of becoming a commodity product.
- Choose a "creator"—a cultural leader who gives the company an aesthetic point of view.
- Hire eclectically: Hire collaborators with different cultures and past histories in order to balance rigor with emotion.
- Lead emotionally: Engender passionate dedication through vision and freedom.
- Build for the long haul. (Creativity requires a lifetime commitment.)

The "Zero Defect" Defect

In early 2003, just 36 hours before the official establishment of the U.S. Department of Homeland Security, I gave a talk to many of the leaders of this new government agency.

My mantra to those assembled:

RAISE THE "100 PERCENT AGAINST ZERO DEFECTS" FLAG. RAISE IT … AND FLY IT PROUDLY.

That flag, which flies at Eglin Air Force Base, traces its roots to Colonel John Boyd, the revolutionary military strategist … whom some have called the most original strategic mind of the past thousand years. Startling, Revealing Anecdote about Boyd: He once told an Air Force general that he (the USAF general) wasn't killing enough pilots in training!

Boyd understood the perils of insisting on "Zero Defects." "Zero Defects" is great—in a known environment. But it is Death Itself … in ambiguous surroundings. And it is Death Itself to … New Dreams.

Problem with "zero defects": No "bold" failures, no "grand" successes. PERIOD.

THERE IS NO ESCAPING THAT LOGIC. NONE.

Dream Metrics: Beyond (Way Beyond) "Zero Defects"

Our tour guide, Mr. Longinotti-Buitoni, insists that "zero defects" and other such sterile measures of "quality" are but a starting point. His measurements of choice:

- "Love at first sight."
- "Design for the five senses."
- "Development to expand the Main Dream."
- "Design so as to seduce through the peripheral senses."

To which I say: YES. YES. YES. And YES.

design

experiences-plus

Do I fully understand all of that? *No!* But then, I've never created a Starbucks ... or a Victoria's Secret ... or a Ferragamo ... or a Ferrari ... or a Harley-Davidson. (Or a reborn and re-invented "BROWN"/UPS.)

But think about it. Think about an aspect of your business ... a clunky procedure, say, that begs to be turned into a Dream Come True. Then apply Longinotti-Buitoni's Measurement No.1: "Love at first sight."

Makes sense to me. For a "product" or a "service." For a business process. For a training course. As well as for a new product or a new marketing campaign.

Next, apply Longinotti-Buitoni's other dream metrics ...

"Design for the five senses"!

"Expanding on the Main Dream"!

"Seduce Through the Peripheral Senses"!

Once More, With Feeling (Damn It)

In the business world, one of the most widely used measures of Quality or Customer Satisfaction is ... "exceeds expectation."

OH, HOW I DESPISE THAT PHRASE.

Suppose you attended the seventh game of the Western Conference NBA play-offs in June 2002. You watched the Los Angeles Lakers war with the Sacramento Kings. Let's say you went with a good pal. On the way out of ARCO Arena, you're shaking with the emotional afterglow of the contest. Do you turn to your pal, and say, "My, my, George, that round-ball contest certainly 'exceeded expectations.' "

OF COURSE YOU DON'T UTTER ANY KIND OF SILLINESS LIKE THAT.

DREAM WEAVING

Two telling quotations from a pair of master ... "dream weavers":

Judy George, of Domain Home Fashions: "We do not sell 'furniture' at Domain. We sell dreams. This is accomplished by addressing the half-formed needs in our customers' heads. By uncovering these needs, we, in essence, fill in the blanks. We convert 'needs' into 'dreams.' Sales are the inevitable result."

Martin Feinstein, of Farmers Group: "No longer are we only an insurance provider. Today, we also offer our customers the products and services that help them achieve their dreams, whether it's financial security, buying a car, paying for home repairs, or even taking a dream vacation."

design

experiences-plus

You
SCREAM!
You
SHOUT!

Expletives ignite the air!

Adjectives and adverbs of the most extreme nature rip the sky asunder!

This was an ... Extraordinary Moment.

This was an ... Extraordinary Event.

(To have been present to see it was ... dare I say it? ... a Dream Come True!)

I am an unabashed ... Business Lover. I believe that enterprise ... can be ... Wildly Creative. Can provide ... Extraordinary Experiences ... for our Employees ... for our Suppliers ... for our Customers.

I believe in "emotion."

I believe in "experiences."

I believe in "dreams."

I believe in language. *Extreme* language. *Emotional* language. Language that ... *Engages You*. That makes you ... *Take Off*.

I
believe in
"dreams."

Dog Days

You might think …. given my preference for "up" language … that I am always "up" myself.

But no. I do have totally crappy days when I can barely get out of bed. On those days I force myself up and go on long rambles with my dogs. For me, the *dog experience* beats even the finest psychopharmaceuticals.

Then … I will get on with it. I force my all-down self back into the fray—not to "finish a project" or "prepare a speech," but to *transform* a project or a speech into a (potentially) transforming experience for someone else.

My greatest fear is that … at the end of the day … I will not have done stuff that mattered. That I will not have made the world … a little better.

So, between my dogs and the possibility of producing "experiences that matter" (that scintillate!), I muddle through. And a funny thing happens: When I re-ignite my enthusiasm, other folks invariably respond in kind.

Message: Enthusiasm begets enthusiasm. Technicolor words beget Technicolor responses.

Message:

ENTHUSIASM BEGETS ENTHUSIASM. TECHNICOLOR WORDS BEGET TECHNICOLOR RESPONSES.

The "Feel" of Dreams: If You Build It ...

If you can get comfortable with words like "dream" and "dreamketing" ... then you can get comfortable with other "un-business-like" words. Words like ... COURAGE.

The product development and marketing expert Doug Hall provides, in an e-missive that he sent me, a brilliant finale for the last two chapters:

"The Internet is the most effective profit killer on Earth. It stimulates a TRUE FREE MARKET—and a REAL free market is the most dangerous of marketplaces for companies selling the SAME OLD STUFF. To those with COURAGE, free markets are great—they help kill off the deadwood competitors who don't have the Courage to Change—making way for them to LEVERAGE their DRAMATIC DIFFERENCE into profitable growth!"

Hats off to ...

SCINTILLATING EXPERIENCES.

DREAMKETING.

HOT WORDS.

CAPITAL LETTERS.

COURAGE.

And to hell with ...

"Exceeding expectations" and "Zero Defects"!

Dreams!

Entirely new possibilities!

Incredible Imaginings!

I DARE YOU TO ENTER THE "DREAM" BUSINESS ... THE "ENTIRELY NEW POSSIBILITIES" BUSINESS ... THE "INCREDIBLE IMAGININGS" BUSINESS.

Will you take me up? Join Dreamers Un-Anonymous? Those Courageous Souls ... willing to Pursue the (Increasingly Possible) Impossible Dream?

INTO THE VALLEY OF DREAMS

My excuse for falling in love (yes, at first sight) with the notion of "incredible imaginings" and "impossible dreams"? Answer: my 25-plus years in Silicon Valley. Where Davids have again and again humbled Goliaths ... only to become, practically overnight, vulnerable Goliaths themselves.

A land of drama. And of dreams (and, yes, nightmares) come true.

In Silicon Valley, *I fell in love*. With Steve Jobs. With Scott McNealy. With Larry Ellison. With people who were ... larger than life. That is: people who had ... DREAMS.

TOP 10 TO-DOs

1. *Stretch out.* Put your business vocabulary to the test. Make it s-t-r-e-t-c-h. Learn to say "Dream Fulfillment" with a straight face, a stout heart, and Absolute Commitment.

2. *Quit the "common" market.* Study Longinotti-Buitoni's list of common products. And study ... even closer ... his list of Dream Products. Now: Put yourself on the right side of that divide.

3. *Zone out "zero."* Troll through your company policies and practices, and banish every vestige of "Zero Defect" thinking ... which, for dreamers everywhere, is a *nightmare.*

4. *Measure for pleasure.* Introduce new and bold metrics in your organization. Example: "How are you doing on the 'love at first sight' scale?"

5. *Go long.* Manage your company, financially and otherwise, for the long haul. A dream isn't built in a day. Or a fiscal quarter.

6. *Surprise and surpass.* Ask yourself, "What explains the gap between 'Dream' and 'common'?" Answer No.1: A Dream *startles* you. Hence your goal must be ... Business-as-Unusual.

7. *Change course.* Turn your all-too-"common" training course into ... not just a fabulous "learning experience" ... but a transformative Dream Experience. (Why not? Damn it!)

8. *Take five.* Flex your "Dream" muscles by learning to "design for the five senses." If you can see it, hear it, smell it, and feel it ... well, then you may just have something.

9. *Scream to dream.* Make the experience that you offer a high-decibel affair. A shout-at-the-top-of-your-lungs affair. Remember: This is most definitely *not* ... a time for understatement.

10. *Capitalize (on) your passion.* Be like Doug Hall (and humble old me), and exhibit your exuberance through a not-so-judicious use of UPPER-CASE LANGUAGE.

COOL FRIEND: Scott Bedbury

Scott Bedbury was senior vice president of marketing at Starbucks from 1995 to 1998. Previously, he spent seven years as head of advertising for Nike, where he launched the "Just Do It" campaign. Below are remarks that he made on the occasion of publishing his book, **A New Brand World: Eight Principles for Achieving Brand Leadership in the Twenty-First Century** *(2002).*

What I love about a brand as organizing principle is how, when it's properly understood across an organization, it can inform and inspire everyone in terms of how they should do what they do, not just what the end goal is at the end of the year on some stock price, some EPS target, some market share number, or some competitor they want to kill. Great companies look *beyond* those metrics to what it is they want their brand to stand for and how it should be perceived and felt by the world that exists inside and outside their company. If a brand is meaningful to consumers and attracts great people to champion it, a lot of the heavy lifting in terms of creating strong numbers is done.

* *

[I]t's not enough to have a great product or service anymore. The world is full of products and services that work. You have to take stock of how your brand makes consumers *feel*. This is not just about your product or service, but about your brand—the sum total of all images that they hold in their head about your company, whether they are legitimate images or not. Great marketers know that consumer perception is reality, unless you work hard to change it.

* *

The "Just Do It" campaign took stock of how people felt. Everyone wanted to be in better shape, to take more control of their lives. We just gave them a little encouragement. For women the campaign was especially powerful. Through the same campaign we demonstrated that we respected what it was like to be a working woman with a lazy husband, a lazy boss, perhaps with kids in daycare and no time to work out. Nike's "empathy" print campaign reached out to them, acknowledged them with a wink as if to say, "Hey, we know life's tough. But we understand the challenge you're up against, and we think that getting in shape might be part of the solution." That's a long-winded way to explain some of the creative strategy behind it, but that's in essence how the campaign became one of the most powerful—and subtle—messages in corporate history.

* *

[W]hen we did that campaign ["Just Do It"] we had no idea it would go beyond August of 1988. It ran for three weeks; it had all of about $8 million of media behind it. But the response inside Nike was instantaneous. And remember, too, this was a company that a year earlier had laid off 25 percent of its work force. You could not give Nike stock away just six or nine months before that. So the survivors and walking wounded found real energy and inspiration in that line.

To Nike employees, the "Just Do It" message was pretty simple: *What's past is past. We know what we have to do. Let's just go get it done. Let's kick some ass.* It was remarkable what happened. I remember debuting the campaign at a sales meeting in June 1988. A thousand Nike employees stood on their feet for almost 10 minutes clapping. That was a real turning point for not just the brand but the people who made it what it was, and more important, what it would become in the years ahead.

* *

[W]e all think of Coca-Cola as an American brand. And certainly it has its roots here. But if you probe young people—teenagers and college students—that are so much more connected to the world than we were at their age, they'll say, "Yeah, sure it started in America, but you've got to understand, Coke is the world's brand.

It's everyone's brand." Which to me is perhaps one of the most powerful brand positions you could ever have, that the ownership is far and wide, and it doesn't rely on someone to adopt the values of a different culture or country. Admittedly, Coca-Cola is probably the most recognized American icon on the planet. But it is fiercely owned by others well outside these borders.

* *

I remember walking off a plane from Chicago to Seattle in 1995. In that particular two-city connection there's a Starbucks right opposite the gate where you get on the plane and another one just outside the jetway on the Seattle end. There was an older couple from Chicago deplaning ahead of me that had been sitting near me on the flight. She stopped in front of the Starbucks in the north concourse, turned to her husband and said, "Look, honey, they have Starbucks here, too!"

And I thought, my God, they're drinking Starbucks coffee in Chicago, and they thought it was theirs, you know? Even though most people know that Starbucks came from somewhere else, they adopt the one near them. So when you ask people, "Where is your Starbucks," they don't even blink about the use of the word "your." They say, "Well, my Starbucks is"—because they have made it part of their neighborhood. ... I can only think of a few other brands that have pulled this off—to become a globally owned brand. And in a time when the world needs a few more unifying concepts rather than dividing ones, it would be great to see brands create experiences that are relevant no matter where you are.

* *

We didn't do any traditional research in the way of pre-testing advertising or even product pre-testing at Nike. A lot of lab work but nothing in front of focus groups, at least in the seven years I was there. We did—in lieu of that—get very close to consumers. We didn't jump in front of them in focus groups or other qualitative environments and say, "What do you think of this line?" or "What do you think of this commercial?" We would spend hours just getting to understand the world they live in, and then very slowly and methodically move it to a discussion about sports and fitness, then to a discussion about footwear and apparel, then to brands, and then ultimately to Nike.

* *

Products come and go, you know? The brand is the thing that exists above and beyond all that. The physical manifestation of brand is a really big misconception.

Another misconception is that people think branding equals advertising or branding is marketing, and that it's the marketing department's job to do the branding. The fact is, branding is everyone's job. Great brand development initiatives nearly always include marketing, but they may also have a profound impact on how the human resource or sales function at a company works.

* *

[D]o a brand audit. That is where you find out what the leadership thinks of the brand, as well as other levels of management, right down to entry-level employees. Brand audits should also include your core customers, your light customers, the ones that hate you, and then maybe the customers you want that don't know you really exist. I did this for a large architectural firm a few years ago and found that the firm's principals had one view of what the brand was and that the young architects that were beginning to really drive the image of the company had a different view. And we had to manage that gap.

And believe me, every company has those gaps, because companies are ultimately human, and we're all different. Now it's one thing to address those gaps with external communication to try and change opinion. But if you don't change it internally first, I don't recommend doing anything externally. Today, more than ever, brands have to walk the talk. If they don't, there's no point in pouring a lot of money into expensive mass marketing. Once the brand is defined and understood inside, developing the tools to change outside opinion is a whole lot easier and a lot more effective.

5

AT THE SUMMIT OF DESIGN: BRANDING FROM THE HEART

Contrasts

Was	Is
Good product	Great "buzz"
Reliable	Unique
Excellent	Memorable
Serves a function	Tells a story
Satisfies a need	Fulfills a dream
What you see is what you get	What you imagine is what you get
Customers own it	Customers use it to shape their identities
"Damn good food"	"Place to be seen"
"Drives smooth"	"Makes a statement"
"Processes my data"	"Helps me make meaning"

!Rant

We are not prepared ...

We acknowledge the unique power and value of "effective branding" in our ever more ethereal economy. • And yet it remains the rare institution that truly grasps what it means to be **TOTALLY, RELENTLESSLY BRAND-DRIVEN.** • **THAT MUST CHANGE.** • **NOW.**

We persist in seeing a "brand" as the "external image" of a company, or of a product or service. • Instead, we must learn that **branding goes straight to the heart** (and comes straight *from* the heart) of an enterprise. • Bottom Line: **EFFECTIVE BRANDING IS FAR MORE INTERNAL THAN EXTERNAL.**

!Vision

I imagine ...

A 22-person Training "Department" embedded in a 700-person Division of Big Co. It is known as the Best-in-Industry at Sales Training. • **YES: THE ABSOLUTE BEST ... AT ITS HYPER-SPECIALTY.** • This "inconsequential" training department offers courses globally, via the Web, and becomes a **No-bull Profit Center and Source of Corporate Recognition**—perhaps even the tail that wags much of the divisional dog.

SAFARI SUNSET
Naturally Caffeine-Free Rooibos Blended
with Stimulating Spices and Lemon

RED
TEA

AFRICAN ROOIBOS HERB

The REPUBLIC of TEA

Natural, Unbleached Tea Bags ❖ Net Wt. 2.03oz (57.6g)

"...Tea Revolution."

Tea Time!

When it comes to branding, my friends Ron Rubin and Stuart Avery Gold get it! They are the honchos of the Republic of Tea. In their book, *success@life*, Ron and Stuart write: "As Ministers of The Republic of Tea, our not-so-covert mission is to carry out a Tea Revolution."

I love that.

Simply love it!

(Don't you wish they were your Big Bosses?)

"Our free and open immigration policies," the Republic of Tea duo continue, "welcome all who wish to flee the tyranny of coffee crazed lives and escape the frazzled fast paced race to stay in one-place existence that it fuels. In our tiny land, we have come to learn that coffee is about speeding up and losing sight, while tea is about slowing down and taking a look. Because tea is not just a beverage, it is a consciousness altering substance that allows for a way of getting in touch with and taking pleasure from the beauty and the wonder that life has to offer."

You might find all that to be a wheelbarrow load of crap. I think instead of wheelbarrows filled with gold.

My point: "All that" gets at the Heart of Branding. The Essence of the Brand Promise. Something that you ... *Care About*. Something that ... *Matters*. Something that you will ... *Stand For*. Something that, perhaps, 270 people who work for you will care about. (And wouldn't that be ever so delightful?)

design

branding from the heart

BRANSON ON BRANDING
Virgin Group Founder and Brand Maestro Extraordinaire Richard Branson: "The idea that business is strictly a numbers affair has always struck me as preposterous. For one thing, I've never been particularly good at numbers, but I think I've done a reasonable job with feelings. And I'm convinced that it is feelings—and feelings alone—that account for the success of the Virgin brand in all of its myriad forms."

And "myriad" is precisely the right word. In a business world where "conglomerate" has rightfully become a maligned term, Branson has performed his Bright Red Virgin Magic in everything from air travel to financial services to the record business. An exceptional story. Based on an unadorned love affair with Branding.

And based on a "sense of fun," on "cheekiness," and on ... *Design*. See Chapter 1: "Design: The Soul of New Enterprise."

Identity Crisis

"The increasing difficulty in differentiating among products and the speed with which competitors take up innovations will assist the rise and rise of the brand," write New Zealand–based marketers Gillian Law and Nick Grant.

"Products from the major competing companies around the world will become increasingly similar," Wally Olins writes in his book *Corporate Identity*. "Inevitably, this means that the whole of the company's personality, its identity, will become the most significant factor in making a choice between one company and its products and another."

Yes. Branding is more important than ever. There are "brilliant" product or service offerings in almost any category you can name. But while being brilliant (putting out good stuff at a competitive price) remains important, it is now merely a starting point ... not the end game.

What's the point? What's the purpose? What ... at heart ... are you made of?

That—and that alone—is what Branding is all about.

Branding is so bloody obvious. When one has an inspiring "identity" ... life gets a whole lot simpler. The problem is, an Identity that Inspires ... is insanely hard to inculcate ... and insanely hard to maintain. On the other hand, the rewards for getting it right can be worth billions, if not hundreds of billions, of dollars in Market Capitalization. (Just ask the folks at Nike or Coke or The Body Shop or Virgin or Harley.) Plus the pride of knowing that what you're doing has Meaning.

WHAT'S THE POINT?

BRAND VALUE: WHEN IT RAINS, IT POURS

Tom Asacker, marketing guru: "Salt is salt is salt. Right? Not when it comes in a blue box with a picture of a little girl carrying an umbrella. Morton International continues to dominate the U.S. salt market, even though it charges more for a product that is demonstrably the same as many other products on the shelf."

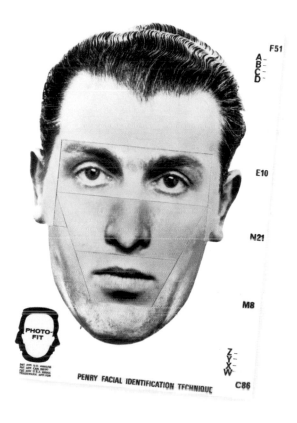

Frequently Un-Asked Questions

Branding. I believe in it.

Insanely.

I believe in "branding"—for myself. As an individual. As a small company owner.

I believe in branding—for you. As a Junior Staffer in the Purchasing Department of Giant Co. Or as a ("mere") waiter in a family-style restaurant. Or as a housekeeper in an 800-room hotel.

I'm befuddled by branding. (It's confusing.)

I'm impressed by branding. (It's powerful.)

I'm turned on by branding. (It's fun.)

Most of all, I care about branding. (It ... Matters.)

Hence I believe ...

Branding is simple.

Branding is impossible.

Branding is *not* about marketing tricks. It *is* about answering a few simple (and yet *impossible*) questions:

WHO *ARE* YOU?
WHY ARE YOU HERE?
HOW ARE YOU *UNIQUE*?
HOW CAN YOU MAKE A *DRAMATIC DIFFERENCE?*

And ... most important ...

WHO *CARES*?
(DO *YOU* CARE?)

Who *Are* You? (I Really Wanna Know)

The top management of a Giant American Company invited me to speak with them. They had experienced a couple of decades of exceptional growth, but growth seemed to be slowing. Employee morale, surveys showed, was slipping a bit, resulting in higher than usual turnover. Their formerly awesome customer service ratings were a bit wobbly. No, the world hadn't come to an end, but it was suddenly (to them) "uncertain." And a brass-knuckled competitor with an investment cache to die for made the issue even more worrisome and urgent.

I studied like hell. Talked to customers. Talked to

design

branding from the heart

THAT'S THE SPIRIT
In this chapter, I have *not* set out to write a "guide to branding." Others have already done that better than I could.

This chapter is a Screed about the Spirit of Branding. The Heart and Soul of Branding. The Fire-in-the-Belly of Branding. Frankly, I think there are

too many "guides" in the ever-expanding world of business books and not enough tracts on ... Matters of Spirit.

131

WHO CARES?

(Do you care?)

vendors. Talked to front-line employees. I had but three hours to spend with the company's Top 50. The first half was to be a presentation; I'd parade my "insightful" PowerPoint slides for 90 minutes. Then we'd talk for the second half of the "show."

As usual, I was suffering pre-presentation insomnia. It was 4 a.m. The speech would begin at 7 a.m. And, yes, I had those slides ready ... 127 of them. I thought. I fretted. And I did something strange: I deleted 126 of the 127 slides. Just one remained. It read:

"WHO *ARE* YOU [These Days]?"

The company had made several acquisitions in the previous half-dozen years. Though I'm a publicly avowed enemy of most big acquisitions, I had no complaint with what this firm had done; each purchase had filled a gaping hole in its portfolio, relative to its powerful competitors. But somewhere ... somehow ... the firm's True Identity seemed to have slithered away, deep into the bushes. So I said: "You can have your fee back if you want, but we're going to spend the entire three hours talking about

WHO ARE YOU [these days]?

'WHO ARE YOU?'"

THE "COME BACK" KID

By the way, my nervy approach worked out brilliantly. The CEO, whom I know well, told me later that this session was perhaps the best meeting that his management team had ever had. "Nobody, Tom, has basically told us that we're full of shit—and don't know who we were. Well done. We might even invite you back."

Postscript: They did.

Post-Postscript: Whew.

(We all survive courtesy of repeat business.)

Mission Control: Why Are You Here?

"You can't just go on forever floating with the tide," writes Danish marketing expert Jesper Kunde, "monitoring the competition and conducting surveys to find out what your customers want now. *What do you want? What do you want to communicate to the world?* ... You need to find out what your company has to offer that will, in some way, enrich the world. And you must believe in that. Believe so strongly that you become unique at what you do."

There's more.

Some companies, Mr. Kunde goes on to write, "equate branding with marketing. Design a sparkling new logo, run an exciting new marketing campaign, and voilà—you are back on course. ... They are wrong. ... The task is bigger, much bigger. It is about the company fulfilling its potential, not about a new logo.

"WHAT IS MY MISSION IN LIFE? WHAT DO I WANT TO CONVEY TO PEOPLE? AND HOW DO I MAKE SURE THAT WHAT I HAVE TO OFFER THE WORLD IS ACTUALLY UNIQUE?

THE BRAND HAS TO GIVE OF ITSELF, THE COMPANY HAS TO GIVE OF ITSELF, AND MANAGEMENT HAS TO GIVE OF ITSELF. ... TO PUT IT BLUNTLY, IT IS A MATTER OF WHETHER [OR NOT] YOU WANT TO BE UNIQUE NOW."

I think that's brilliant.

Branding: It's about ...

MEANING, NOT MARKETING

... about deep company logic, not fancy new logos.

design

branding from the heart

GREEN MEANS (LO)GO

I agree with Jesper Kunde. And yet ...

Sometimes a New Logo can make a ... Dramatic Difference. I think that British Petroleum is one such case. A few years ago, BP launched a campaign to establish a Dramatic Difference within its industry by Going Green. While many people are justifiably skeptical of this move, I believe that this Green Thing is very real—and very potent.

One part of this effort is the introduction of an absolutely stunning new logo. I am struck by how much the logo strikes me when I see it while driving down a street or highway.

If not unique ... WHY BOTHER?

The Best—or Bust: How Are You Unique?

UNIQUE. There is no bigger word. None.

Unique means ... SINGULAR. RIGHT?

"Success," says Tom Chappell, founder of the personal care products company Tom's of Maine, "means never letting the competition define you. Instead, you have to define yourself based on a point of view you care deeply about."

Brilliant.

But even Tom can be upstaged. By the late Jerry Garcia of the Grateful Dead, who said: "You do not merely want to be considered the best of the best. You want to be considered the only ones who do what you do."

The Grateful Dead were precisely that—"the only ones that do what [they] do." They changed the world. (I am a fan, by the way. Not a Deadhead, but a sympathizer.)

If not *unique* ... WHY BOTHER?

design

branding from the heart

(DON'T) FOLLOW THE MONEY

It's surprisingly easy to move from the world of the Grateful Dead to Polly Hill Arboretum on Martha's Vineyard. Stephen Spongberg, who runs this magnificent facility, says, "We're not going to be driven by where we think a funding agency would like to see us go. We're going to build our case about what's important to us ... and then find a funding organization that agrees with us."

What he said, as I see it, is that he is very ... VERY ... clear that he knows how to answer the question "HOW ARE YOU UNIQUE?"

BRANDING: NOT A LUXURY

The stakes in the "uniqueness" game are high. And getting higher.

Michael Silverstein and Neil Fiske, writing in their 2003 book, *Trading Up: The New American Luxury:* "A shipping clerk earning $25,000 a year treats herself to silk pajamas at Victoria's Secret. A dual-income couple earning $125,000 orders a $4,000 Viking range for their townhouse even though the developer offered to throw in a perfectly serviceable generic range at no extra charge. These purchases reflect an important worldwide behavioral shift. Consumers today are willing to pay a significant premium for goods and services that are emotionally important to them and that deliver the perceived values of quality, performance and engagement. But in other categories that aren't emotionally important, they become bargain hunters: a passionate Mercedes driver will shop at Target every weekend; a construction worker who splurges on a $3,000 set of Callaway golf clubs will buy store brand groceries."

It's the Law: How Can You Make a Dramatic Difference?

Doug Hall is the "idea guru" (according to an *Inc.* magazine cover story). A former marketer at Procter & Gamble and now overseer of Eureka Ranch, Doug has guided big corporation team after big corporation team to stunning new product breakthroughs. Aiming to translate his big-company insights to the world of small business, he wrote a wonderful, meticulously researched book, *Jump Start Your Business Brain*. (In a foreword to the book, I called it … SUPERCALIFRAGILISTICEXPIALIDOCIOUS. Reason: It uses a ton of "hard data" to support a slew of brilliant "soft" ideas.)

At the book's heart are what he calls the three "laws" of "marketing physics."

Law #1: Overt Benefit.

What is the product or service's "One Great Thing"? (One or two "great things" is far better than three or more "great things." When you get to three or more … you just confuse the consumer. Hard data supports the point.)

Law #2: Real Reason to Believe.

Does the organization Really and Consistently Deliver that "One Great Thing"?

Law #3: DRAMATIC DIFFERENCE.

The Hard Data Scream: *Dramatic Difference in a product or service offering makes a very Dramatic Difference in Top- and Bottom-Line Success.* Alas, Hall reports, damn few (Very Damn Few!) executives get it.

Consider this scenario: A few hundred consumers are asked to evaluate a potential new product or service. They confront two questions: "How likely are you to *purchase* this new product or service?" and "How *unique* is this new product or service?"

UNIQUENESS

=

THE
EMOTIONAL
CONNECTION

The consumers' responses to those questions are intriguing—but not nearly as intriguing as the way the company's top executives have responded to the survey. Execs (no exceptions in 20 years, according to Hall!) give 95 percent to 100 percent weighting to results from the "intent to purchase" question, and a 0 percent to 5 percent weighting to the "uniqueness" consideration.

Fact: THEY GET IT ASS-BACKWARDS.

Trust the data. The predictor of future success, relative to the questions posed, is ... UNIQUENESS. (Not "intent.") Because ...

UNIQUENESS = THE EMOTIONAL CONNECTION.

RISING SIGN

Even in Japan, long known for its stable domestic market, competition is intensifying. And the winners of that competition are increasingly cut from a different-from-the-past stripe. Less emphasis solely on Cost and Quality and Consistency. More focus on ... Dramatic Difference.

And one key differentiator? Design!

From an August 2004 piece in the Nikkei *Weekly: "Low-price strategy is now outdated. Firms gaining more market share are fueled largely by the incorporation of design and unique functions into popular products."*

Who Cares? (You'd Better Care!)

When Bob Waterman and I penned *In Search of Excellence*, back in the early 1980s, the received dogma of the time had reduced "management" to a dry, by-the-numbers exercise. Bob and I roamed the business landscape, looking at companies that worked—and what we saw departed from the ruling norms. What we saw was "soft," by the Harvard Business School standard. It was all about *people* and *engagement in work* and *love of quality* and *entrepreneurial instinct* and *values worth going to the mat for.*

The "surprising" (surprising, that is, in 1982) Waterman-Peters Mantra:

SOFT IS HARD. HARD IS SOFT.

In other words: It's the "numbers" stuff that's abstract and lifeless. *(Hard Is Soft.)* It's the "people" and "passion" stuff that moves mountains. *(Soft Is Hard.)*

To our delight (and surprise), the world took note—not because of our scintillating prose, but because the competitive situation demanded it. Our "wild stuff" has now become commonplace:

Engage your folks.

Make things that are cool and that work.

Stick your neck out.

This is all a long-winded way of saying that ... PASSION (aka EMOTION, aka CARING, aka DRAMATIC DIFFERENCE) ... has

STICK YOUR NECK OUT.

EMOTION NOTION. HEART SHARE

Swedish professors Kjell Nordström and Jonas Ridderstråle, writing

in *Funky Business:* "In the funky village, real competition no longer revolves around market share. We are competing

for attention—*mind share and heart share.*"

finally become recognized as *the* Staple of Successful Business. Not a poor second cousin to the "quant stuff" that business schools still thrive on.

Verb Power: Go Where the Action Is

TBWA/Chiat/Day CEO Jean-Marie Dru is the most provocative marketer I've run across in recent times. His recent books—*Disruption* and *Beyond Disruption*—are among the best business books I've read in many a year. Jean-Marie makes this extraordinary point:

"Apple *opposes*, IBM *solves*, Nike *exhorts*, Virgin *enlightens*, Sony *dreams*, Benetton *protests*. ... Brands are not nouns but verbs."

I admit it. I'm absolutely enamored of Dru's idea. *It's driving me batty.* I don't know exactly what to do with it. But I know that I need to do ... *something important* ... with it. (Dru's idea, by the way, ties brilliantly into the "experience" stuff and the "dream" stuff I talked about earlier.)

Everyone (*everyone!*) must put himself/herself this short and simple question: *What is your verb?* What verb describes the (Unique and Dramatically Different) Value-Added offering that you create in your ... Training Department ... Logistics Department ... Purchasing Department ... Finance Department ... New Product Development Department ... Engineering Department ... Information Systems Department. In your 18-table restaurant. Or your four-person financial advisory firm?

To the quantitative bigots, this reeks of fluff. To me (a Reformed Quantitative-ist), it sounds like the Billion-Dollar Question.

design

branding from the heart

EMOTION NOTION: ONLY CONNECT

Scott Bedbury, who played a lead role in the branding of both Nike and Starbucks (Wow!), explained his philosophy to *Fast Company* magazine: "A great brand taps into emotions. ... Emotions drive most, if not all, of our decisions. ... A brand reaches out with [a] powerful connecting experience. It's an emotional connection point that transcends the product. ... A great brand is a story that's never completely told. A brand is a metaphorical story [that] connects with something very deep—a fundamental appreciation of mythology .... Stories create the emotional context people need to locate themselves in a larger experience."

A Promise Is ... The Premise

I frequently take my clients through a little drill. I call it the "Brand Promise Exercise." It goes like this:

1. WHO ARE WE? (a) Write a two-page

short story (with a Scintillating Plot Line) about ... Who We Are. (b) Now boil it down to one page; better yet, capture it as a Poem or Song. (Yes, including the Brand Promise Song of the Finance Department!) (c) Reduce it to 25 words. (Or perhaps 10.) **(Or 5.) (Or a verb.)**

_____

2. THREE WAYS. List three ways in

which we are ... UNIQUE to our clients.

_____

_____

_____

3. DRAMATIC DIFFERENCE.

State ... Precisely ... the ... One Great and Dramatic Thing ... that distinguishes us from our competitors. In 25 words. (Or less.)

_____

_____

_____

**EMOTION NOTION:
STORY TIME**

Rolf Jensen, head of the Copenhagen Institute for Future Studies, writing on ... the Call of Stories: "We are in the twilight of a society based on data. As information and intelligence become the domain of computers, society will place new value on the one human ability that can't be automated: emotion. Imagination, myth, ritual—the language of emotion—will affect everything from our purchasing decisions to how well we work with others. ... Companies will thrive on the basis of their stories and myths. ... Companies will need to understand that their products are less important than their stories."

"NIKE sells the experience
of using Nikes."

design

4. WHO ARE "THEY"? (a) Explain
who each Major Competitor is. In 25 powerful, precise,
flattering ... and truthful ... words. (Or less.) (b) List
Three Extremely Distinct "Us" vs. "Them" differences.
(No bull here. No cutting corners.)

_____

_____

_____

_____

_____

_____

design

5. TRY IT ON TEAMMATES.
Test the results of this survey on teammates and other
colleagues. Talk about the survey. Argue about it. Scream
about it. Seriously. At length.

6. TRY IT ON CLIENTS.
(a) Test the results of this survey on a Friendly Client.
(b) Test them on a Skeptical Client.

7. TRY IT ON ...
EVERYONE ELSE. Test the results
of this survey on a cross-section of people in the
organization (starting with checkout and stock clerks).

branding from the heart

WORTH THE BOTHER
Marketing guru Jesper
Kunde provides this report
of an exchange with a
client from an ostensibly
"mundane" business:

Client: "But we're
nothing like Nike! We sell
paper clips, notch grinders
and 9mm bolts. Who can
be bothered?"

Kunde: "The whole
world can be bothered ...
if you brand them well.
Nike does not actually sell
shoes. ... Nike sells the
experience of using Nikes,
the feeling of being a
winner, and they condense
the whole message into
the three words: Just Do It!
... It is a question of
being the only one, of
offering your market
something unique."

Promises to Keep

I once spoke at a seminar for a large financial services company. I listened to the CEO give a fine address. (Truly, it was damn good—and I'm a damn good judge by now.) He laid out a Vision. (And don't forget to capitalize that V in "Vision"!) It made sense. But it was a stretch—which is the point. A big stretch, at that. I spoke immediately after the Big Dude had finished. And I warned ... and challenged ... the several hundred people in the room.

I said that the Brand Promise (New Vision) was important. And it made all sorts of sense to me. But I added that unless those in the room Totally Bought Into It ... then the whole exercise was ... a Crock.

"Does this 'Brand Promise' make sense to *you*?" I asked. "As individuals? In your daily work? With your clients? Is it a Genuine, Dramatic, Inspiring Departure from the Past? Does the new 'story line' give you, yes, goose bumps?" And if not, I said to them, "Please ... PLEASE ... Raise Holy and Unmitigated Hell with the CEO ... and tell him why the products and services that you offer do *not* add up to the Scintillating (Dramatically

BRAND CALISTHENICS: MARK MY (AND YOUR) WORDS

There are dozens of ways to improve your branding muscle tone.

Jesper Kunde has the people who work for him write an essay on "Who we are." I like that. (An essay goes beyond "programs.")

In my case, the *discipline* of branding became real when I decided to write text for a series of bookmarks that would accompany some publications of mine. I thought it was a great idea. That is, I thought so ... until I sat down to write the copy for these

things. I had about 15 words to summarize ... WHO I WAS, and WHAT I HAD BEEN DOING FOR THE LAST 30 YEARS, and WHY IT OUGHT TO MATTER TO HUNDREDS OF THOUSANDS OF READERS.

(Gulp!)

Different) Brand Promise Story (New Vision) that he has just laid out."

Maybe I won't be invited back. Maybe I pissed him off. He had gone on at length about how the "top team" had "worked hard" on the vision. Top team, shlop team. Who the bloody hell cares? A "Vision" matters only ... if the PFC (Private First Class) ... Buys Into It ... and Will Run into Professional Machine-Gun Fire because of his Belief in that Vision (Inspired Brand Promise).

Yes, branding *is* about the logo ... the slogan ... the marketing campaign ... the advertising. But, in the end, branding is about ... CREDIBILITY.

Do the 99.99 percent of your people who Work in the Trenches ... Buy the Act? Do they Live It? (With Vigor.) Do they Convey It? **(With Passion.)**

BRAND CALISTHENICS: ELEVATOR ... GOING UP!
In the Brand You training that my company conducts, we find the most useful exercise is having clients concoct a one-eighth-page Yellow Pages ad ... for *themselves*. ("Essence of Tom" ... in 25 words. Or some such.)

Many tell us that it's the toughest professional task they remember ever doing.

Likewise, in our WOW Project training, the centerpiece is preparing "The Elevator Speech," a 90-second spiel that you'd use to get support for your project ... if you found yourself alone with

your Big Boss for a 20-floor ride.

These exercises aim for one thing: CAPTURING THE ESSENCE OF THE BRAND PROMISE—ITS DRAMATIC DIFFERENCE AND TOTAL COOLNESS—IN A VERY SUCCINCT AND VERY COMPELLING FASHION.

design

branding from the heart

Brand Leadership: An Easy Act to Follow

Branding and "Leadership" are Siamese twins. The Brand Promise is a vibrant, living, changing saga called ... Things We Care About. It requires Passion—the kind of passion that only Inspired Leaders can project.

Franklin Roosevelt, America's Brand Manager of Dignity and Freedom during the Great Depression ("The only thing we have to fear is fear itself") and World War II ("December 7, 1941, a date which will live in infamy"), said, "It is necessary for the President to be the nation's number one actor."

In fact, all of Leadership *is* an Act! It's an act that involves ... Conveying the Brand Promise via Demonstrated High Conviction in Pursuit of Great and Noble Purpose.

That Great and Noble Purpose can be Democracy, Peace, and Prosperity. Or it can be the provision of the finest Cajun cuisine in New Orleans, the most imaginative business processes in the mortgage-banking industry, or the Best-Ever Employee Memorial Day Picnic.

In any event, leaders of all descriptions must wholly embody that sense of purpose. Indeed, they must ... look the part. As Adlai Stevenson once said, "You can't lead a cavalry charge if you think you look funny on a horse." In fact Roosevelt—who, in the wake of his bout with polio, was certainly no horseman—was careful never to be seen in an incapacitated state. Instead what people consistently saw in him was a supreme air of tenacity and confidence during a time of mortal trial. Roosevelt's cigarette holder said it all. Like Churchill's cigar, it was an Oscar-quality prop.

design

branding from the heart

BRAND CALISTHENICS: HAIKU = HIGH COUP

Consider taking a course in creative writing. Business writing is typically stilted and insipid. Keep in mind Rolf Jensen's remark about stories and myths: We need training in story, myth, and metaphysics far more than we do ... another accounting course.

Case in point: I recall the story of a brilliant Japanese exec who devoted his long flights around the world not to working through a briefcase full of memos and financial reports, but to constructing haiku—those miraculous 17-syllable poems. Maybe your next "business" course ought to be on haiku?

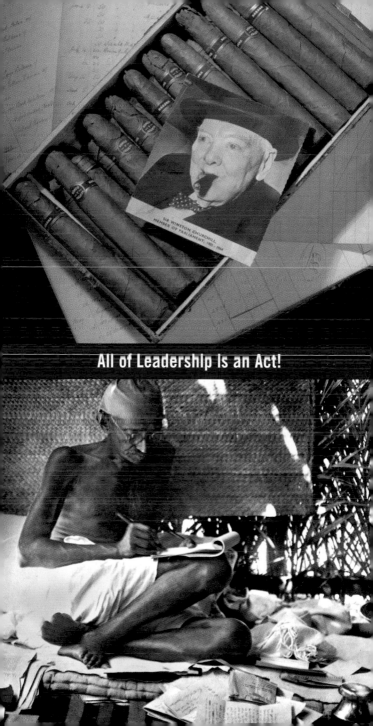

All of Leadership Is an Act!

However, the Oscar goes to Mohandas Gandhi, who dressed brilliantly for the part of non-violent nation builder and chose his main prop, the humble spinning wheel, with care. Said Gandhi: "You must be the change you wish to see in the world."

BRAND IDENTIFICATION

Great enterprise leaders take on the "role" (read: "brand") of their company or product. Thus:

Steve Jobs	*... is ...*	*Apple Computer*
Bill Gates	*... is ...*	*Microsoft*
Larry Ellison	*... is ...*	*Oracle*
Scott McNealy	*... is ...*	*Sun Microsystems*
Andy Grove	*... is ...*	*Intel*
Sam Walton	*... is (was) ...*	*Wal*Mart*
Richard Branson	*... is ...*	*Virgin Group*
Anita Roddick	*... is ...*	*The Body Shop*
Oprah	*... is ...*	*Oprah*
Giorgio Armani	*... is ...*	*Armani*
Charles Schwab	*... is ...*	*Charles Schwab*

Brand Leadership: A Great Story to Tell

"Leaders achieve their effectiveness chiefly through the stories they relate. ... In addition to communicating stories, leaders *embody* those stories," writes Harvard leadership guru Howard Gardner in *Leading Minds: An Anatomy of Leadership*. "Stories [have] identity. ... [They are] narratives that help individuals think about and feel

---

HIGHER HOPE—OR JUST "HIRED HELP"?

I'd been at my Martha's Vineyard house for about a week. And was heading back to Vermont. On the way to the Vineyard Haven-Woods Hole ferry, I drove past an A&P grocery store. (Now a Stop & Shop.) On an outer wall I spotted a big banner: A&P Fun in the Sun Store.

I surely don't have any problem with that aspiration. (I think it's great, to tell the truth.) But then I thought about the innards of the store. (Pretty ordinary.) And I thought about a characteristic checkout clerk. I thought about a stocking clerk. Does that stocking clerk or checkout clerk really believe ... that he or she is an ... Insanely Great Contributor to ... the "Fun in the Sun Store"?

Answer: I doubt it. (Seriously.) Which led me to this reflection: Great Slogans and Great Logos and Great Brand Promises are ... TOTAL, EGREGIOUS, IMMORAL, COUNTER-PRODUCTIVE BULLSHIT. UNLESS ...

UNLESS ... The "Talent" ... those stock clerks & checkout clerks ... Buy In. One Hundred Percent. Or if not 100 percent, at least 92.58 percent.

who they are, where they come from, and where they are headed. [They] constitute the ... single most powerful weapon in the leader's arsenal."

GREAT LEADERSHIP IS ... GREAT STORYTELLING.
CHURCHILL. DE GAULLE. LINCOLN. ROOSEVELT. REAGAN.

Great Branding is ... a Great Story. The Coca-Cola saga. The UPS saga. The IBM saga. (And the incredible story of that wonderful four-table deli in San Francisco.)

Can you, as a Brand Leader (of a 4-person operation or 4,000-person corporation), convey Your Story succinctly? Can you convey it in a Powerful Way? Is it Believable? Exciting? Mind-Altering? To employees? To vendors? To customers? To the media?

Thus, we have ... leadership as *Acting* and leadership as *Storytelling*. But Real Leadership—especially inspired Brand Leadership—is about something more. It's about ... well, I'll just say it: "Leadership is all about ... LOVE."

That's not a "soft" statement. IT IS THE ULTIMATE HARD STATEMENT. Leadership is all about ... Winston Churchill and Mohandas Gandhi and Albert Einstein & Martin Luther King, Jr., and Caesar Chavez and Gloria Steinem and Charles de Gaulle and Theodore Roosevelt and Franklin Roosevelt and Thomas Jefferson and John Adams and Alexander Hamilton and Susan B. Anthony. Brand Leadership is all about ... Passion and Enthusiasm and Engagement and Commitment and Determination to Make a Difference and Shared Adventures and Outrageous Failures and an Insatiable Appetite for Change.

That's *the* Gandhi secret. *The* FDR secret. Every effective leader's secret. Alas, it remains (mostly) a secret.

Where's the Fire?

I had a troubling conversation with a Very Senior Executive. Someone I know reasonably well. We were talking about a Monstrous Strategic Initiative that his firm was launching. It concerned nothing less than a redefinition of the enterprise. We talked intensely for an hour and a half. Some of the programs that he mentioned were as exciting as the dickens.

But during those 90 minutes, I "heard" (sensed) virtually no emotion. I thought of meetings that I've had with the likes of Scott McNealy (Sun Microsystems). Steve Jobs (Apple). Anita Roddick (Body Shop). Mickey Drexler (The Gap). Rich Teerlink (Harley-Davidson). Their language—especially their "subtle" (like a freight train!) body language—wouldn't have been the same as that of this Very Senior Executive. At all. When you spend time with them ... you can ... Feel the Fire.

Sure, branding requires "programs" and "strategic initiatives"—but it comes from the Gut. From the Heart.

In other words: *You Gotta Believe! You Gotta Vibrate!*

When you pull this "brand thing" off, there is a level of engagement that is ... Purely Visceral.

(TO DENY IT IS INSANITY.)

Pure, Raw Emotion.

Pure, Raw Commitment ... to do "The Brand Thing" ... because ... it's the "Life Transforming Thing to Do."

(BECAUSE IT IS WHY YOU ARE HERE.)

YOU GOTTA

BELIEVE!

YOU GOTTA

VIBRATE!

get

How do we instill this quality? How do we hire for it? How do we promote it? How do we spread it throughout the ranks of top management? How do we keep it alive from generation to generation?

Attention Must Be Paid: The Heart of Branding

I hate Dilbert.

I h-a-t-e Dilbert.

I laugh at *Dilbert* ... but I hate it ... because it is a comic strip that exudes unabashed cynicism. And I hate cynicism. I am past 60 ... and going on 65 years of age. I don't have all that many years to go. I would like to make those years count.

I care.
Passionately.

And people who don't care ... appall me.

In any walk of life. Street sweeper. Top engineer at Cisco Systems.

I care.
I hope you care.

I lived in Silicon Valley for over three decades. There is one guy who has inhabited and helped form that Valley of Dramatic Dreams ... one guy there whom I take a shine to more than anybody else: Steve Jobs. Steve is ...

design

branding from the hea—

LOVE MARKS THE SPOT
In branding, passion (or lack thereof) works both ways. You must exude passionate commitment to your brand identity. And that's because the name of the game is to ... instill passionate commitment ... in your customers.

Kevin Roberts, CEO of Saatchi & Saatchi, writing in his 2004 book *Lovemarks: The Future Beyond Brands:* "Trustmarks come after brands; Lovemarks come after Trustmarks. ... Think about how you make the most money. You make it

when loyal users, heavy users, use your product all the time. ... So having a long-term Love affair is better than having a trusting relationship."

The One Who Really Made the Revolution Happen. His company, Apple, was the engine of all else that followed. Here is my favorite Steve-ism:

"Let's make a dent in the universe."

How sweet that is.

Most of us won't "make a dent in the universe." But we at least can try.

It's simple.
It's impossible.
It demands your attention.
Your attention to ...
Who are *we?*
Why are we here*?*
How are we unique*?*
How can we make a
Dramatic Difference*?*
Who cares*? (Do* we *care?)*

That is the Heart of Branding. Because Branding is ultimately about nothing more (and nothing less) than *Heart*. It's about Passion ... What You Care About. It's about What's Inside ... what's inside you, what's inside your department, what's inside your company.

There's more to it. (Of course.) But if you "get" this part of BRANDING ... then you've got its ... HEART.

BRANDING FROM THE HEART

Let's review. Branding from the heart ... from the top:

REAL Branding is ... Personal.

REAL Branding is about ... Integrity.

REAL Branding is ... Memorable.

REAL Branding is about ... both Consistency and Freshness.

REAL Branding is a ... Great Story.

REAL Branding ... Matters. (To employees. To customers. To suppliers.)

REAL Branding is about ... Passion and Emotion.

REAL Branding is about ... Why We Get Out of Bed in the Morning.

REAL Branding ... can't *ever* be faked.

REAL Branding is ... a 24/7, All-departments, All-hands Affair.

TOP 10 TO-DOs

1. *Ask away.* Pose and keep posing the sorts of question that "they" don't teach you in business school. Example: Why are you here? (See full list above.)

2. *Identify yourself.* Look within ... deep within ... and figure out What You Are Made Of. Again: *When one has an inspiring "identity" ... life gets a whole lot simpler.*

3. *Keep your word.* Write down the particulars (implicit or explicit) of your company's Brand Promise. Keep them at your side and in your heart.

4. *Talk it up.* Become the Bard of Your Brand ... the master storyteller who carries the brand's "design specs" deep in your soul and spreads its story far and wide.

5. *Shrink it down.* Hone your brand message until it fits smoothly into a 90-second "elevator pitch." (Do it, for real ... with a stop-watch, if need be.)

6. *Re-verb-erate.* List all the verbs you can think of—all the *action* words—that apply to your brand. Then winnow your list down to ... just one verb. Remember it. Say it. Be it.

7. *Be a class "act."* Rehearse your Brand Leadership thing with all the care and performative zeal of a ... master thespian. Mantra: Look the part.

8. *Obey the laws.* Take a cue from Doug Hall, and measure your brand against his three laws of "marketing physics." Key "legal" term to remember: DRAMATIC DIFFERENCE.

9. *Stay soft.* Cultivate a flair for the so-called "soft stuff"—the not-easily quantifiable heart and soul and blood and sinew of Who You Are. (Hint: You are not Your Numbers.)

10. *Design from on high.* Treat branding and design as what they are. Namely: Two ways of harnessing *passion* within enterprise. Two facets of the same exercise in ... *soul-making*.

INDEX

AUTHOR'S ACKNOWLEDGMENTS

It required a far-flung virtual village to make this book. Here I wish to note a few "essential" residents of that village:

Michael Slind, editor, and Jason Godfrey, designer, both continued the sterling work that helped make my previous book (*Re-imagine!*) so sharply compelling. In adapting that book to make this one, they both achieved the noble feat of reinventing the project from within.

Stephanie Jackson, of Dorling Kindersley, pushed and pushed—and charmed and charmed—this book into being. Also at DK, Peter Luff used his sense of visual panache to help produce a "small" book with big impact, and Dawn Henderson applied her editorial talent deftly, creatively, and crucially at every stage of the project.

Erik Hansen served in his usual role of "project manager," though that term fails to capture the unique mix of doggedness and nimbleness that he brings to all of my publishing ventures. Cathy Mosca attended to details of authorial execution and factual accuracy with her typical vigilance.

My thanks to them all.

PERMISSIONS

Grateful acknowledgment is made to the following:

Rodale Inc.: Synonyms for "experience"from *THE SYNONYM FINDER* © 1978 by Rodale Inc. Permission granted by Rodale Inc., Emmaus, PA 18098. Available wherever books are sold, or visit www.rodalestore.com

FOR THE CURIOUS ...

Source notes on the stories and data cited in this book are available online (www.tompeters.com/essentials/notes. php). Also on the Web are complete versions of the Cool Friends interviews excerpted in the book (www.tompeters. com/cool_friends/friends.php).

PICTURE CREDITS

Picture Researcher : Sarah Hopper
DK Picture Library : Richard Dabb

The publisher would like to thank the following for their kind permission to reproduce their photographs;
(Abbreviations key; t=top, b=below, r=right, l=left, c=centre, a=above, tl=top left, tr=top right, bl=below left, br=below right).

10: Science Photo Library/David Mack; 14: akg-images/Erich Lessing; 17: Herman Miller Inc.; 18: courtesy of S.C.Johnson; 24: courtesy of Gillette Group; 29: Corbis/ Tom Wagner; 34: Corbis/Jon Sparks; 38: Apple Corps Ltd (l); courtesy of BMW (r); 39: courtesy of Gillette Group (b), Sony Corporation (t); 46: Science Photo Library/ David Mack; 53: Corbis/Michael Prince; 56: Science Photo Library/Scott Camazine; 60: Corbis/George D.Lipp; 63: Corbis/Bettmann; 66: Science Photo Library/David Mack; 75: Corbis/Peter Turnley; 76: Corbis/Michael S.Yamashita; 79: courtesy Starbucks (b), Guinness & Co. All rights reserved (t); 84-85: courtesy of Chrysler; 87: Getty Images/Foodpix; 90: The Art Archive/Bill Manns; 100: Science Photo Library/David Mack; 104-105: Corbis/William Manning (t); 106-107: Corbis/William Manning (t); 108-109: Corbis/Nogues Alain (bl); Corbis/ Wally McNamee (tl); 109: Corbis/Cardinale Stephane (tr); courtesy of Google (cra), Courtesy of Virgin (crb), courtesy of Centrino (br); 110-111: Corbis/William Manning (t); Corbis/Bill Robinson (b); 112-113: Corbis/ William Manning (t); 114: Corbis/William Manning (t), Getty Images/John Lund (b); 116: Corbis/William Manning (t); 122: Science Photo Library/David Mack; 126: courtesy of Republic of Tea; 129: Corbis/ Bettmann; 142: Corbis/Martin Hughes; 147: Corbis/Hulton-Deutsch Collection (b); Nadia Mackenzie/Elizabeth Whiting Associates (t).

All other images © Dorling Kindersley. For further information see: www.dkimages.com

Hear Tom Peters Live with Red Audio (TM).

ABOUT THE AUTHOR

The Economist *called Tom Peters the Uber-guru.* BusinessWeek *labelled him "business's best friend and worst nightmare."* Fortune *tagged him as the Ur-guru of management, and compared him to Ralph Waldo Emerson, Henry David Thoreau, Walt Whitman, and H.L. Mencken. In an in-depth study released by Accenture's Institute for Strategic Change in 2002, he scored second among the top 50 "Business Intellectuals," behind Michael Porter and ahead of Peter Drucker.*

In 2004 the compilers of Movers and Shakers: The Brains and Bravado Behind Business *reviewed the contributions of 100 business thinkers and practitioners, from Machiavelli to J.P. Morgan to Jack Welch. Here's how the book summarized Tom's impact: "Tom Peters has probably done more than anyone else to shift the debate on management from the confines of boardrooms, academia, and consultancies to a broader, worldwide audience, where it has become the staple diet of the media and managers alike. Peter Drucker has written more and his ideas have withstood a longer test of time, but it is Peters—as consultant, writer, columnist, seminar lecturer, and stage performer—whose energy, style, influence, and ideas have shaped new management thinking."*

Tom's first book, coauthored with Robert J. Waterman, was In Search of Excellence *(1982). National Public Radio in 1999 placed the book among the "Top Three Business Books of the Century," and a poll by Bloomsbury Publishing in 2002 ranked it as the "greatest business book of all time." Tom followed* Search *with a string of international best-sellers.* A Passion for Excellence *(1985, with Nancy Austin),* Thriving on Chaos *(1987),* Liberation Management *(1992),* The Tom Peters Seminar: Crazy Times Call for Crazy Organizations *(1993),* The Pursuit of WOW! *(1994);* The Circle of Innovation: You Can't Shrink Your Way to Greatness *(1997), and a series of books on Reinventing Work—The Brand You50, The Project50, and* The Professional Service Firm50 *(1999). In 2003 Tom joined with publisher Dorling Kindersley to release* Re-imagine! Business Excellence in a Disruptive Age. *That book, which aims to reinvent the business book through energetic presentation of critical ideas, immediately became an international No.1 bestseller.*

Leadership guru Warren Bennis, the only person who knows both Tom and Peter Drucker first-hand, told a reporter, "If Peter Drucker invented modern management, Tom Peters vivified it." Indeed, throughout his career, Tom's overriding passion has been passion. Among his current passions: women as leaders; the supreme role of design in product and service differentiation; the creation of customer experiences that rival a Cirque du Soleil performance; and the enormous, underserved markets represented by women and by Boomers.

Born in Baltimore in 1942, Tom resided in Northern California from 1974 to 2000 and now lives on a 1,600-acre working farm in Vermont with his wife, Susan Sargent. He has degrees in civil engineering from Cornell University (B.C.E., M.C.E.) and in business from Stanford University (M.B.A., Ph.D.). He holds honorary doctorates from several institutions, including the State University of Management in Moscow (2004). Serving in the U.S. Navy from 1966 to 1970, he made two deployments to Vietnam (as a Navy Seabee) and survived a tour in the Pentagon. He also served as a senior White House drug-abuse advisor from 1973 to 1974. From 1974 to 1981, he worked at McKinsey & Co., becoming a partner and Organization Effectiveness practice leader in 1979. Tom is a Fellow of the International Academy of Management, the World Productivity Association, the International Customer Service Association, and the Society for Quality and Participation. Today, he presents about 75 major seminars each year (half of them outside the United States), and participates in numerous other learning events, both in person and on the Web.

SAY IT LOUD – THE ESSENTIALS MANIFESTO

They say...   I say...

They say...	I say...
Sure, we need "change."	We need REVOLUTION. NOW.
Your (my) language is extreme.	The times are extreme.
I am extreme.	I am a realist.
I demand too much.	"They" accept mediocrity too readily.
Brand You is not for everyone.	The alternative is unemployment.
Take a deep breath. Be calm.	Tell it to Wal*Mart. Tell it to China. Tell it to India. Tell it to Dell. Tell it to Microsoft.
What's wrong with a "good product"?	Wal*Mart or China or both are about to eat your lunch. Why can't you provide instead a Fabulous Experience?
The Web is a "useful tool."	The Web changes everything. Now.
We need an "initiative."	We need a Dream. And Dreamers.
Great Design is nice.	Great Design is mandatory.
You (I) overplay the "women's thing."	The minuscule share of Women in Senior Leadership Positions is a Waste and a Disgrace and a Strategic Marketing Error.
We need a "project" to explore "new markets."	We need Total Strategic Realignment to exploit the Women and Boomer markets.
"Wow" is "typical Tom."	"WOW" is a Minimum Survival Requirement.
We like people who, with steely determination, say, "I can make it better."	I love people who, with a certain maniacal gleam in their eye, perhaps even a giggle, say, "I can turn the world upside-down!"
Let's speed things up.	Let's transform the Corporate Metabolism until Insane Urgency becomes a Sacrament.
We want recruits with "spotless records."	Those "spots" are what defines Talent.
We favor a "team" that works in "harmony."	Give me a raucous brawl among the most creative people imaginable.
We want "happy" customers.	Give me pushy, needy, nasty, provocative customers who will drag me down Innovation Boulevard at 100mph.
We want to partner with "best of breed."	Give me Coolest of Breed.
Happy balance.	Creative Tension.
Peace, brother.	Bruise my feelings. Flatten my ego. SAVE MY JOB.
Plan it.	DO IT.
Market share.	Market Creation.
Basic black.	TECHNICOLOR RULES!
Conglomerate and Imitate.	Create and Innovate.
Improve and Maintain.	DESTROY and RE-IMAGINE!